# Spring 89

# Buddhism and Depth Psychology
## Refining the Encounter

## A Journal of Archetype and Culture

Spring 2013

SPRING JOURNAL
New Orleans, Louisiana

# SPRING: A JOURNAL OF ARCHETYPE AND CULTURE

Nancy Cater, Editor-in-chief
Polly Young-Eisendrath, Guest Editor

Jungiana Editor: Riccardo Bernardini    Film Review Editor: Helena Bassil-Morozow
Book Review Editor: Emilija Kiehl

## Advisory Board

*Spring* is the oldest Jungian psychology journal in the world. Published twice a year, each issue explores from the perspective of depth psychology a theme of contemporary relevance and contains articles as well as book and film reviews by a wide range of authors from Jungian psychology, the humanities, and other interrelated disciplines.

Founded in 1941 by the Analytical Psychology Club of New York, *Spring* was edited by Jane Pratt until 1969. With the 1970 issue, James Hillman became the editor of *Spring* and moved it to Zürich. When Hillman left Zürich and became the Dean of Graduate Studies at the University of Dallas in 1978, he transferred the editing and publishing of *Spring* there. It was edited in Dallas until 1988 when Hillman and *Spring* moved to Connecticut. Hillman retired as Publisher and Senior Editor of the journal in 1997. From 1997 until 2004 *Spring* remained in Connecticut and was edited by Charles Boer. *Spring* moved its offices to New Orleans, Louisiana in 2004 and has been edited by Nancy Cater there since.

Cover Image:
Detail of "Three Cranes Flying in a Misty Landscape". Anonymous (Japan). 19th century (Edo-Meiji Period). Ink and colors on silk mounted on paper and brocade. Current location Walters Art Museum.

Editorial and production assistance:
Drummond Books, drummondbooks@gmail.com
Cover design, typography, and layout:
Northern Graphic Design & Publishing, info@ncarto.com

*Spring is a member of the Council of Editors of Learned Journals.*

Spring Journal™, Spring: A Journal of Archetype and Culture™, Spring Books™, Spring Journal Books,™ Spring Journal and Books™, and Spring Journal Publications™ are all trademarks of Spring Journal Incorporated. All Rights Reserved.

# CONTENTS

## BUDDHISM AND DEPTH PSYCHOLOGY: REFINING THE ENCOUNTER

# HUMOR, HEALING, AND HELPING

# LAGNIAPPE

# FILMS

# BOOKS

# GUEST EDITOR

**Polly Young-Eisendrath, Ph.D.**, Jungian Analyst, Psychologist, author; Clinical Supervisor, Norwich University, Northfield, Vermont; Clinical Associate Professor of Psychiatry, University of Vermont, Burlington, Vermont; and in private practice in central Vermont. She is chairperson of the non-profit "Enlightening Conversations: Buddhism and Psychoanalysis Meeting in Person" that hosts conferences in cities around the USA. She has published many chapters and articles, as well as fourteen books that have been translated into more than twenty languages. Her most recent books are *The Self-Esteem Trap: Raising Confident and Compassionate Kids in an Age of Self-Importance* (Little, Brown: 2008) and *The Cambridge Companion to Jung: New and Revised*, of which she is co-editor with Terence Dawson (Cambridge University Press: 2008). She is working on a new book, tentatively called *Love Broken Open*. Polly is a long-time practitioner of Zen Buddhism (since 1971) and Vipassanā (since 1998) and a mindfulness teacher. www.young-eisendrath.com.

# INTRODUCTION

POLLY YOUNG-EISENDRATH

North American Buddhism has celebrated its fiftieth birthday. Large established American Buddhist centers—such as San Francisco Zen Center, Rochester Zen Center, and Karmê Chöling Shambhala Meditation Center—have been teaching students and training teachers for more than forty years. American Buddhist magazines and other Buddhist media and educational outreaches have had extraordinary impact on popular culture, so much so that His Holiness the Dalai Lama is now a celebrity who attracts massive crowds to his teachings in America. Although only about one percent of the US population identifies themselves as "Buddhist" in surveys such as the US census, almost everyone in a public forum in cities like New York, San Francisco, and Los Angeles will raise a hand when I ask "How many of you practice some form of mindfulness?" The development of Buddhism in North America has been rapid, easy, and surprising, considering that in my childhood almost no one had any knowledge of the religion or its practices, and what knowledge was available was at best fuzzy and at worst entirely inaccurate. The spread of Buddhist influences is even more remarkable because the religion opposes proselytizing. Buddhism spreads through actual interest in its ideas and practices.

The American practice of depth psychology is about one hundred years old—the American Psychoanalytic Association dating back to 1911 and the C. G. Jung Institute of New York to 1912. The development of depth psychology in North America has been far more problematic and contested than the development of North American Buddhism. Although the various schools—from Freudian, Jungian, and Adlerian to interpersonal, object relations, modern, self psychology, ego psychology and relational—have long established their training institutes and journals, and although the Freudian approach had a brief acceptance in medical schools, the major purveyors of mental health practices in America refuse to embrace the legitimacy of psychoanalysis in any of its forms. And this continues despite its well-established credentials, theory, and scientific evidence base. While it is beyond my aim here to offer an explanation for this apparent mismatch between the theories and practices of psychoanalysis and the mental health establishment in North America, I would simply note that the time, patience, and reflective attitudes required of patient and therapist in the psychoanalytic therapies—as well as the demands made by psychoanalysis on conventional thinking—are not remarkably different from those required for Buddhist practice. But psychoanalysis is conducted in the marketplace of mental health practices whereas Buddhism does not seem, at least initially, to demand a financial commitment.

Additionally, the professional institutes and organizations sponsoring the training and development of depth psychology are fraught with long-standing destructive schisms and conflicts. The underlying psychoanalytic "hermeneutic of suspicion," so-called by philosopher Paul Ricoeur, has traditionally encouraged an attitude of doubt about one's own and others' motives that has sadly led to an atmosphere of mistrust.[1] Psychoanalysts seem endlessly preoccupied with whether someone with a slightly different training is "really a psychoanalyst." Also, there is no common language among practitioners who use the "talking cure" to explore unconscious expressions, dynamics, and themes within the unique setup of a two-person intimate, but professional, relationship.

Even the term *psychoanalysis* is disputed. It was originally coined by Freud to name his school and method while Jung chose the term *analytical psychology* for his approach, and some practitioners continue to believe that a line was drawn in the sand between the two. Over the decades, however, the term *psychoanalysis* has survived in the popular domain to refer to the form of psychotherapy that relies on analyzing unconscious dynamics occurring both in everyday life and in the relationship between therapist and patient—often called transference and countertransference—expressed in unintentional affective communications and dreams. Consequently, I and others among my Jungian colleagues have chosen to call ourselves "Jungian psychoanalysts." This clarifies that we belong to that circle of therapists who analyze unconscious dynamics as the major means of healing. And so, in this introduction, I will use the term *psychoanalysis* as the general rubric under which are located all psychotherapies that focus on the transformative power of analyzing unconscious dynamics and meanings.

Although Buddhism has its own specialized terms and schisms, in its long 2,600-year history, it has not by and large produced the deep and frustrating animosities that continue to plague contemporary psychoanalysis in North America. In my view, this difference is mostly due to the fact that Buddhism requires its practitioners to train themselves in practices of mindfulness, kindness, friendliness, and "right speech" which are to be used in speaking with others and with one's self. These awareness practices permit one the freedom to pay attention to destructive emotional impulses without necessarily expanding them into a narrative that captures the imagination. Overall, the practices encourage an openhearted, kind, and friendly attitude toward oneself and others and discourage opinionated prejudices and biases.

Even though a lot of hierarchy exists in many forms of Buddhism, there is also a deep acknowledgment that practices and ideals develop "from warm hand to warm hand" instead of being inculcated by authority outside one's experience. My first Zen teacher told me early on, "No one can get between you and the consequences of your actions (karma). Only you can know what you are doing." North American psychoanalysts, on the other hand, tend to their specialized concepts and institutes very seriously. Small differences are magnified and judged. So it seems that psychoanalysis has something to learn from Buddhism in relation to cultivating an attitude of interest, discovery, and kindness that extends outside the consulting room, especially to colleagues and fellow travelers.

On the other hand, North American Buddhism has something to learn from psychoanalysis when it comes to understanding and making skillful use of a two-person or group relationship to an authoritative teacher and idealized practices. Buddhist teachers unconsciously tend to rely on what Freud called an "unobjectionable positive transference" and what later analysts have called an "idealizing transference." This refers to the elevating of the teacher or practice or ritual to a position of idealized power and authority that is unrealistic and split off from ordinary aspects of being human. When a person or group is thought to be without flaws, mistakes, weakness, or shortcomings, then idealization is holding sway. Idealization tends to be accompanied by the power of suggestion, under which authority is followed blindly or unrealistically. Buddhist ceremonies, special costumes and customs, and rituals tend to enhance the power of suggestion and idealization, to the Western eye at least, in such a way that can lead to harmful power dynamics or problematic behaviors especially if the authority figure is said to be "fully enlightened."

The papers in this volume help us refine the conversation between contemporary North American Buddhism and contemporary North American psychoanalysis. While I believe we all agree that we can benefit from getting to know one another's practices better, we have a long road ahead to see clearly what we are speaking about and to apply our various wisdoms where they are most needed.

## My Background Briefly

My own background includes a lot of practice and study in both Buddhism and psychoanalysis. Buddhist exposure came first and was foundational in my initial attempt to see into the nature of my subjective experience. In 1971, just out of college, I took formal vows to become a Zen Buddhist in the tradition of Philip Kapleau. In 1998, after Rōshi Kapleau's serious illness and aging meant he officially became a friend and no longer a teacher, I became a student of Shinzen Young, a teacher who combines Vipassanā with Zen teachings. Eventually I also became a mindfulness teacher in his tradition. Both of my teachers are Americans trained in Asia, concerned about helping their students ground Buddhist teachings in American culture.

On the other side of the coin, in 1986 I became a Jungian analyst after eight years of training and have filled many roles (including ten years of teaching and research in a Freudian psychoanalytic hospital) and written many books, chapters, and articles on Jung's work and on the conversation between Buddhism and psychoanalysis. My home on the side of a mountain in Vermont now includes both a small retreat center and a clinical suite where I have a full-time therapeutic practice. Many of my analytic patients are practicing Buddhists who are also psychotherapists; some have been teachers, but most are students.

In all of the many ways I engage with the interface between Buddhism and psychoanalysis, I am sensitive to the potential for misunderstanding. In both traditions, there are many specialized terms and subtle ideas that easily become distorted. I have worked hard at being an able translator between the traditions. Although there are specialized psychoanalytic terms used in the papers that follow, it is the Buddhist ideas that are likely to be less well understood by a typical reader. Also, many Buddhist terms are imprecise or encompass several meanings simultaneously. And so, I spend most of my effort here introducing the Buddhist terminology used in the papers that follow. Over the decades, I have found my way through the maze of terms. I will offer my own definitions here without reference to other sources.

### BUDDHIST NAMES, CONCEPTS, AND TERMINOLOGY

To begin, I would like to mention the three forms of Buddhism that are most frequently practiced now in North America: Vipassanā, Zen, and Tibetan Buddhism. Vipassanā (a word that is sometimes translated as "insight" and sometimes as "seeing things as they really are") is linked to the earliest Buddhist practices, the Theravāda tradition (meaning "teaching of the elders"). All of these forms of Buddhism originated in India although they developed for centuries in other cultures with which they are now identified. Vipassanā comes in different varieties, mostly from Southeast Asia, especially from traditions that reside in Burma, Sri Lanka, and Thailand. Zen is a Buddhist practice that developed in China and later in Japan, Vietnam, and Korea before it came to the West. The legendary (probably not factual) founder of Zen (or Chan) Buddhism in China is someone called Bodhidharma (who died around 532 if he lived). He allegedly came from India to practice in a cave in China and had a famous meeting with a Chinese emperor. Zen exemplifies Mahāyāna Buddhism (the great vehicle) and recognizes our profound unity with all beings and our commitment to liberating all. The third popular North American form is Tibetan, a branch of Vajrayana Buddhism (the diamond vehicle) that emphasizes skillful means for reaching all beings and the integration of all forms of practice into a universal way. Starting roughly in the third century, Buddhism developed as a central part of Tibetan culture until 1950 and the Chinese invasion, followed by the Tibetan revolt against the Chinese and the Dalai Lama's escape to India in 1959. Since then, Tibetan teachers have gradually come out into the Western world, establishing communities in India and abroad.

To introduce some basic terms shared among Buddhist schools, I begin with *Buddha, Dharma,* and *Sangha.* The Buddha refers both to the human Buddha (Siddhartha Gautama who is also called Shakyamuni Buddha) and to the quality of fully awakened awareness. *Buddha* sometimes means the awakened mind itself. That there was an ordinary human being who was awakened to cosmic consciousness gives confidence to those who are attempting to awaken to that same experience now. *Dharma* refers both to the teachings of the Buddha and also to the natural spiritual laws of our existence. The Buddha taught Buddhadharma, his own approach to unpacking our natural conditions in order to become liberated from entangling desires and fears while we are alive. *Sangha* refers to both the community of the Buddha's followers—the community of practitioners—and to all "Noble Ones" who are dedicated to awakening and wisdom. On one hand, Sangha means our fellow travelers on the Buddhist path, and on the other hand it means anyone who is nobly dedicated to awakening and wisdom.

Sometimes the Dharma is also called "the marks of existence." They are qualities of reality uniformly true for everyone. In the language of Pali (a language close to the one the Buddha spoke), they are three: *dukkha, anicca,* and *anatta. Dukkha* is frequently translated as "suffering" although that translation is misleading and inadequate. *Dukkha* is a term that has no simple equivalent in English. It refers to a quality of off-centeredness, like a wheel riding off its axle or a bone out of its socket. *Dukkha* is felt as anguish, suffering, anxiety, stress, confusion—whether it emerges from negative or positive sources. The second aspect of Dharma is *anicca,* a word readily translated as "impermanence" or constant ceaseless change. Impermanence may be perceived as negative (I am aging) or positive (even though I am in pain, I know the pain will change and lessen). The third condition, *anatta*—in Sanskrit, anātman or the negation of Atman—refers to a quality that is often called no-self or emptiness in English. Again, this term is hard to translate into English and often becomes confused with the existential philosophy of nothingness or the void. And yet, the Buddhist term refers to the quality of no-thingness—not to the some-thingness of nothingness. I have, for the time being, embraced the words *embedded* and *contextualized* to express the inter-being that *anatta* points to: everything, including ourselves, is absolutely embedded in contexts within which we arise moment to moment. *Anatta* shows our non-separation from the entire universe in which we abide. The Buddhadharma, then, helps us to see into and experience the nature of *dukkha*, *anicca*, and *anatta* in order to free ourselves from greed, hatred, and ignorance—especially our ignorance of *anatta*. All paths of Buddhism are designed to help us free ourselves from the conditions and attitudes that bind us to various kinds of unhappiness and delusion.

Other terms that may confound you, in the following papers, have to do specifically with Zen Buddhism, a form of practice that originated in China in the sixth century. Zen is a form of Mahāyāna Buddhism that emphasizes the Bodhisattva ideal and compassion. The term *Zen* comes originally from the Sanskrit word for sitting meditation and absorptive states. *Dyana* (meaning "sitting meditation" in Sanskrit) is transformed into *Chan* in Chinese and *Zen* in Japanese and related words in Korean and Vietnamese. Zen emphasizes meditation, especially sitting and walking meditation. *Zazen* is the term for meditation practice. Some Zen students work with "koans": unsolvable puzzles that stop the mind from prematurely conceptualizing or controlling experience. One koan, mentioned in several papers here, is called the Genjokoan and was originally formulated by the founder of the Soto Zen School in Japan. This koan offers views of the self in a paradoxical and implication-filled way. The founder of Soto Zen is Eihei Dōgen (1200–1253), a Japanese monk who was born in Kyoto and traveled to China to study with masters there and then returned to Japan and started Soto Zen at the temple now called Eihei-ji.

Whereas in Vipassanā, students are usually given group instructions and a clear set of practices—on which they are questioned and tested by their teachers—in Zen, students typically work intimately with a teacher who observes them carefully in all their activities at the monastery or center as well as questions them in personal interviews. In Vipassanā, the relationship with a single teacher is less important than mastering practices. But in Zen, student and teacher form a lifetime bond. Many Zen practices require deep trust in one's teacher and that trust may be initially encouraged through idealization. Many practices in Tibetan Buddhism similarly involve a close personal relationship with an idealized teacher whose very presence is meant to awaken the student's motivation for enlightenment. Students of Tibetan Buddhism also practice guru yoga in which they venerate their teachers as deities although that veneration is also deconstructed as part of the practice, revealing insights into *anatta*. All of these relationships with teachers, ideals, and practice are aimed at the same goal: awakening to the actual truth of the deep reality of an abiding love, support, and wisdom—and then sharing this awakening with other beings through helping and teaching.

In some schools, especially in Zen, awakening is understood as the wiping away of delusions and fears from an underlying Buddha Mind or Buddha Nature. In such teachings, beings (human and others) are seen as having naturally awakened minds that are covered by myriad obstacles and destructive tendencies. When these obstacles are cleared away, the being is awakened. Over centuries, Buddhists of all schools have debated the nature of mind. In some schools, Buddha Mind or Buddha Nature sounds like some-thing instead of no-thing. One of the most important teachings on this issue was written by the second-century Indian Buddhist philosopher Nāgārjuna, who argued that Nirvana (enlightenment) and Samsara (delusional existence) are both impermanent and no-thing. From Nāgārjuna's point of view, no state is eternal or unchanging in this world. An "enlightened being," then, is not permanently enlightened nor is Buddha Nature a "thing" to be counted on. His teachings and the paradoxical instructions that have surrounded them for centuries provide many arenas in which practitioners engage in spiritual debate and discovery.

Finally, I want to mention one last teaching cited in papers here: it is called Trikāya and refers to three different registers or "bodies" in which we exist simultaneously—remarkably similar to some psychoanalytic teachings (Lacan, Sullivan, and Jung come to mind immediately). The first is the register of conventional reality in which we share language, culture, and perceptions of objects, opposites, time, and space; this is called *nirmanakaya* in Sanskrit. The second is the register of dreams, fantasies, visions, psychoses, and other idiosyncratic forms of both divine and demonic natures; this is called *sambhogakaya*. The third register is a formless realm that cannot be named or expressed or symbolized. It is the formless source, called *dharmakaya*. We all have access to all three, but tend to get stuck in the first and second, overlooking the transformative no-thingness of the third.

## THE PAPERS

I have organized the papers in a way that I hope will provide a transformative experience for the reader. There are three sections, and to have the richest and most engaging encounter with the papers, they should be read in order. If you want to jump around, you should read at least the first paper in each section to become acquainted with the fundamental ideas and terms that come up in later papers.

In the first section, "Awakening and Insight," you will find papers that help you see into the experience of awakening and tell you something about the path to get there. Also described in these are some ordinary psychological limitations that still plague people after they have glimpsed transcendent reality. In a nutshell, you will see how Buddhist practices focus on developing clarity, concentration, and equanimity with our universal *individual* reality whereas psychoanalytic practices focus on developing clarity and equanimity with the personal habitual emotional dynamics of our everyday relationships with our selves and one another. Buddhism focusses on the universal and psychoanalysis, on the personal.

The first paper, "Light and Dark: Koans and Dreams," by Zen teacher and dream-worker Henry Shukman, gives a clear picture of a dialectic between the process of spiritual awakening through Zen practice and a personal journey through archetypal dreamwork. The second paper, "Settling the Mind Meditation: Subjectivity and Beyond," by psychiatrist, Buddhist practitioner, and psychoanalyst Adeline Van Waning, stems from her participation in the Shamatha Project (with Buddhist teacher Alan Wallace) in 2007, a three-month Buddhist meditation retreat combined with neuroscience research. Van Waning shares with us specific instructions in the practices she learned and her experiences of developing deep concentration and equanimity— as well as their relationship to psychotherapeutic themes and emotional development. "On Being a Zen Psychoanalyst: The Union of Presence,

Meaning, and Intimacy," is by psychoanalyst, psychologist, and Buddhist practitioner Jeffrey Rubin, who gives us a snapshot of working in psychoanalysis from a Zen perspective. "Unconscious and Conscious Meet Self and self: Depth Psychology and Zen Meditation" is by Zen teacher and psychologist Grace Jill Schireson. She writes about the common ground, common aims, and different methods of Zen and analytical psychotherapy. The final paper in the opening section, "Calming the Mind (*An-hsin*): The Early Chinese Zen Buddhism and Psychotherapy" by psychologist, translator, and Japanese scholar Shoji Muramoto, covers some complex and subtle questions about what Western psychologists, compared with early Zen Buddhists, mean by "mind" and "calming the mind." He raises the question of whether we are speaking past one another when we refer to the phenomenological mind of psychotherapy and the transcendent mind of Buddhism.

In the second section, "Idealizing, Suggestion, and Projection," we look more specifically at some of the problems created and addressed by the two practices. Buddhism and psychoanalysis both depend to some extent on an idealizing transference to experts (Buddhist teachers and psychoanalysts) in order to reorient students/patients on deep questions about truth and reality. How does this work? What are the pitfalls? Where can the two traditions learn from each other?

The first paper, "Suggestion and Truth in Psychoanalysis and Buddhism," is by a psychoanalyst new to Buddhism. Psychiatrist and Kleinian psychoanalyst Robert Caper guides us through a labyrinth from suggestion and idealization to direct awareness of truth, and tells us how these developments in psychoanalysis may inform Buddhist practices. Next, "Knowing Our Teachers: Intersubjectivity and the Buddhist Teacher/Student Dyad" opens our eyes to one of the biggest problems with idealizing Buddhist teachers: refusing to confront them when they are suffering from obvious psychological problems that could be readily treated. Psychologist, psychoanalyst, and Buddhist practitioner Pilar Jennings applies contemporary psychoanalysis in situations in which teachers have gone tragically untreated because their students were confused, complicit, or afraid to speak out. "Buddha as Walkaway" examines the ways in which the Buddha's awakening and its aftermath can be applied to treating the problem of scapegoating, in which there is a split between the ideals and the dark underside of a group. Jungian psychotherapist, educator, and Buddhist practitioner Alexandra Fidyk shows us how group analysis can be expanded through mindfulness.

In the third section, "Humor, Healing, and Helping," we apply what we have learned from earlier papers in some precise and specific ways. The section opens with a paper by the South African clinical psychologist and Jungian writer Deon van Zyl: "A Sense of Humor, Enlightenment, and Individuation" draws on Jung, Freud, koans, and jokes to show how humor can bring us suddenly into nondual awareness, face to face with the formless source. The second paper, by psychologist, psychoanalyst, and mindfulness practitioner Melvin E. Miller, gives a visceral sense of koans and the healing capacities of aesthetics when we deeply acknowledge that we are all more wounded than otherwise. Titled "Reflections on Genjokoan, Kintsugi and *Participation Mystique*: Mutual Transformation through Shared Brokenness," this paper skillfully integrates several topics introduced in the first two sections. In "Haiku and the Healing Way," psychiatrist, Jungian psychoanalyst, and writer David H. Rosen shows how the practice of haiku—with its Zen aesthetic and paradoxical silences—has served to integrate aspects of his individuation and spiritual journey in his lifelong search for truth, meaning, and love. The final paper—"Buddhism, Psychoanalysis, and the Care of Homeless People"—is written by Lacanian/ Winnicottian psychoanalyst Deborah Anna Luepnitz, a newcomer to Buddhism. It invites us to enter deeply into the psychoanalytic treatment of a homeless woman through which we can see into the paradox of home/homelessness in light of the Buddha's admonishment to his followers to leave behind their homes and possessions.

This is an extraordinary collection of papers that allows us to examine the realms of human suffering, subjective experience, wisdom, and truth from surprising new perspectives. In my view, this volume introduces a new level of discourse between two contemplative practices—Buddhism and psychoanalysis—that are still coming to know one another and whose cross-fertilization promises a new paradigm of human healing.

## NOTES

1. Paul Ricoeur, *Freud and Philosophy: An Essay on Interpretation,* trans. Denis Savage (New Haven, CT: Yale University Press, 1970), pp. 32–33.

# AWAKENING AND INSIGHT

# LIGHT AND DARK
## KOANS AND DREAMS

### HENRY SHUKMAN

### A MOMENT OF AWAKENING

Many people first get into Zen by reading a book about it, or by meeting a Zen master, or from a general curiosity about meditation. For me it was different.

One afternoon when I was nineteen years old I found myself alone on a beach. As I stared out at the water, I saw that it looked coal-black yet at the same time dazzlingly bright where the sunlight licked over it. I was trying to figure out if it was actually black or blindingly white when suddenly everything changed. It was as if the whole world that I had always believed to be outside me—the phenomenal world—was suddenly not outside me, and never had been. That light on the water was in me. It was me myself. At the same time, it was as if I'd split open too, and my heart was filled to overflowing with a love I couldn't explain or name, yet which was deeply

Henry Shukman has published eight books of poetry, fiction, and memoir, several of which have been Books of the Year in the *Times* (London) and *Guardian*. He has won the Arvon Poetry Prize, *Times Literary Supplement* Poetry Prize, and Arts Council England Writer's Award and has an M.A. from Cambridge and an M.Litt. from St. Andrews University. He is a Zen teacher in the Sanbo Kyodan lineage and is primary teacher at Mountain Cloud Zen Center in Santa Fe, New Mexico (www.santafezen.org). He also has a small practice as an Archetypal Dreamwork therapist.

familiar and precious. It seemed to fill the entire universe as if I was made of the very same substance as the cosmos.

I had never known anything like it. Nothing in my liberal humanist education had prepared me for it. Yet I knew I had just seen an absolute truth of the universe, of who I was, of what it meant to be a human being. The afterglow went on for days. I lived in a world transfigured. In the hours immediately afterward, the sand was unimaginably soft and powdery, and the sea looked like it came straight out of the Bronze Age Aegean I knew from my schoolboy studies of Homer. Everything seemed like it was both real and unreal—like an ancient dream I had had many centuries ago, in another lifetime. A flame of love wouldn't stop burning in my heart. My heart had been swamped, overtaken, overwhelmed by a kind of love I had never known before, yet which was powerfully familiar.

Cut forward ten years. I've been to university, I've worked in various odd jobs, I've begun a life as a writer, having published one book and being in the middle of a second. It seemed that after a rocky start my "career" was beginning to work out. Yet I was unsettled. One major reason for this was that although the experience on the beach had faded into the background, I still couldn't forget it. Whatever it was, it still felt like the most important thing that ever happened to me. But what was it? And how could I get back to it? Sometimes I felt a kind of guilt or dismal failure, because I seemed incapable of recapturing it.

Then I met someone who happened to be a Zen student. One evening she read me a passage of Dōgen, the thirteenth-century Japanese Zen master who founded the Soto Zen sect in Japan. I didn't understand a word of it: something about mountains walking, and mountains not being mountains. But something happened as I listened. Somehow, I knew this man Dōgen understood what I saw on the beach. He was speaking from that incredible world I had stumbled onto. So I got myself trained in *zazen*—Zen meditation—as soon as I could. I also began a long search for my own Zen teacher. Finally, another ten years on, I settled down with a teacher in the Sanbo Kyodan, a Zen lineage that employs traditional koan study.

I came to discover that every koan is about that very reality I glimpsed on the beach. They are about the "essential world"—a world that we can apprehend, but which seems to radically contradict our "dualistic" or everyday view of things. There is indeed another side to everything. Through the course of koan training, and through a series of further plunges into the vast, ever-changing, ever-empty, unitary world of Buddha Nature, different yet similar to the one I'd had on the beach, this world penetrated my psyche more and more, until one day the wall between the two worlds—the everyday world and the world of awakening—came tumbling down in one radical thunder-crash.

Life has been much easier since.

The above is one version of my story. Here is another: I grew up in a ruinous broken home occupied by my siblings, myself, and my depressed mother, who had been abandoned by her husband, my father, in favor of her own first cousin, with whom he set up a home just down the road in our hometown of Oxford, England. In addition to the difficulties of life with a betrayed, depressive, single mother, I spent my childhood encrusted in eczema. The disease was ugly and painful and itched with a fury beyond any number of mosquito bites. I was often in hospital and, when home, was regularly visited by district nurses.

Finally at the age of eighteen I escaped and went away to work in South America, and the eczema lifted like a magic spell. For the first time my skin ceased to cause anguish. It became a thing of pleasure. I could hug without pain, shake hands without shame, and look at people without quaking at the thought of the rashes and gashes on my face and limbs. I also earned some decent money. Then I backpacked with a friend to remote corners of the Andes, seeing things more beautiful than anything I had ever imagined, and wrote my first book, *Sons of the Moon* (Scribners, 1989). Near the end of the trip, I went down to a beach and had that strange moment of union with all things. Then I went home.

Just six weeks after the epiphany by the sea, I pulled up in the English rain outside my father and stepmother's house in Oxford. After a few minutes of awkward conversation in the living room, sitting on a chair and feeling like I was perched over a cliff, I went upstairs to take a warm bath. And there something else happened, in its way as dramatic as the moment on the beach. As I listened to the sound of the plumbing whistling in the fabric of the house and the murmur of the voices coming from downstairs, a terrible familiarity swept over me. This was the nightmare I had grown up in: I had walked right back into it. I seized up in despair and sobbed like I hadn't in years.

All the misery of my childhood, held at bay while I was living through it, tumbled down on me. The person I had started to become, the new hopeful life I was embarking on, seemed to be destroyed and lost, because I had done the worst thing possible: I had come home.

For the next few months I lived in a daze of grief, unable to converse for fear of breaking down. But I couldn't understand it. What was going on? Why so upset? First, a doorway of light opened on that beach; now, a doorway of darkness. It never occurred to me that both doors could possibly lead onto one and the same path.

### The Buddha's Awakening

According to the Pali Canon, when Shakyamuni Buddha experienced his great awakening at the age of thirty-five, it did not come about through grueling ascetic practices. Rather, after several years of mortifying his flesh under the guidance of various spiritual masters, to the point where he had brought himself close to death, he realized three things. First, he wanted to live and therefore took nourishment to restore his constitution. Second, in spite of all his asceticism, he had come no nearer to fulfilling his existential quest. And third, he remembered a time as a child when he had experienced complete happiness, without any special practices at all. Rather than put himself through more deprivation and torture, why couldn't he just be happy like then? So he decided to abandon severe asceticism and instead sit quietly under a banyan tree and let the memory of that childhood moment guide him.

According to Aśhvaghoṣa, who embellished the Pali Canon's stories, the moment in question happened when as a young boy Siddhartha had been watching a man plowing. His nanny had left him in the shade of a rose apple tree at the side of a field, and as he saw the plow's blade cut through the earth, he noticed dozens of insects scurrying for their lives. An overwhelming sadness welled up in him. These little creatures were desperate, and he could feel their pain as if it were his own. Then hard on its heels came an equally overwhelming joy. He suddenly saw that the insects were not just linked to him but were actually part of him: he and they formed a single phenomenon, a single body. That discovery, of a hidden identity with all beings, brought effortless joy. It arose spontaneously from his heart. This moment could surely be labeled a "spiritual experience," a clear apprehension of the *dharmakaya* or Dharma body, the singularity of all phenomena. Yet it came about through feeling—through tenderness, hurt, compassion, love. The path to the spiritual ran through the heart. The heart, the organ of love and pain, was the master key.

A common prejudice holds that spiritual practice is not about feelings: it transcends feelings, it takes us beyond our small self. In a way this is true. But if spirituality is only about self-transcendence— about seeing through the story of "me" that we habitually inhabit—then it runs the risk of cutting us loose from that story so that we no longer take care of the human wounds of self and other. We may become dependent on self-transcendence as a means of avoiding subjective and intersubjective problems. No matter how imaginary the self proves to be, we return to its world. If spiritual or transcendent insight doesn't lead to healing and transformation in our actual daily lives, it is clearly incomplete.

Zen teaching is quite clear on this: the training is not about transcending the self but seeing clearly what the self is, seeing through it and thus becoming less convinced and imprisoned by it. In his Genjokoan, Dōgen says (to paraphrase): first, we see that all is one; then we see that there is no self; then we drop the whole system of self and world and are liberated. After that, we forget all about enlightenment, and let the "flowers fall amid our longings, and the weeds spring up amid our antipathies"—in other words, we lead lives rich in human responses, with our hearts wide open. In the West, Buddhist practice is still very young, having been around for just about fifty years. Nevertheless, perhaps that is old enough to begin to feel a responsibility to move from a simplistic view of enlightenment as transcendence to a more integrated stance of awakening as embracing the subtleties of living responsibly and responsively within our relationships and communities.

### KOANS AND DREAMS: ZEN AND PSYCHOTHERAPY

What is the sound of one hand clapping? What is your original face before your parents were born? Why has the bearded Bodhidharma no beard? In all, there are said to be some 1,700 classical Zen koans. In the Zen line in which I have trained and now teach, we use about

650, nearly all of them recording the sayings and actions of Zen masters from Tang Dynasty China (618–907 C.E.). They are teaching stories with an extraordinary power to bring about a dramatic shift in our experience of self, world, and consciousness. We call this sudden shift *kenshō*—seeing our real nature. If pursued assiduously, koans can thoroughly break our attachment to, release us from enthrallment to, the self-protective sense of "I, me, mine." Zen, if it's anything, is a training in becoming less self-absorbed, less self-centered, but it's really much more than that.

The koan is a short anecdote or story that contains some apparent paradox or enigma that cannot be resolved by the thinking mind. "What is Buddha?" a monk asked Tozan; he replied, "*Masagin*" (three pounds of flax). While it may be possible to work out a conceptual explanation of this koan, the teacher is looking rather for a living embodiment of the koan in the student, who must present it with an action. By surrendering to the enigma of a koan we allow it to take us over and to open us up to an unexpectedly broad field of awareness. By sitting with one koan after another, week after week, and taking each one to the teacher, the barriers between our sense of self and the world around us may be weakened to the point where they crumble altogether, after which we are freed to meet each moment as it arises, with less attachment to outcome and greater compassion.

Yet all this—*kenshō*, koan training, and so on—is only one side of the practice. Zen training opens up a space for another side, less dramatic but equally important. If the first side is sudden, this other is gradual. In a new spaciousness within our experience, gradually we learn to accept ourselves more thoroughly; in doing so we heal the wounds that need healing and become kinder and wiser, more able to function helpfully. At least, that's the ideal.

It was on this side of Zen training that after several years of koan study I started to become interested in my dreams. I was going through a difficult phase in my marriage and was finding my work life stressful. We are multidimensional beings, and healing in certain areas does not imply healing in all areas. Even though Zen might have clarified that I and my world were both inventions, I still wanted some extra help negotiating those inventions. My Zen teacher Joan Rieck Rōshi had done some dream work herself years before, with Robert Johnson and at the Jung Institute in Switzerland, and I was curious about it. From reading Rodger Kamenetz's *The History of Last Night's Dream*, I was attracted to the ideas of the controversial dream worker Marc Bregman. His approach, which he calls archetypal dreamwork, is in some ways analogous to koan work. A story or image (in this case a dream) is used as a means of personal transformation; here, too, there is an authority higher than the personal. In koan training we sit with stories of the masters; in archetypal dreamwork we sit with the stories told by our dreams. While these are not equivalent, the work in both cases involves being prepared to sit with them patiently. In both, there are difficult lessons to be learned about who we really are. Both often involve being open to discomfort. The prick of a koan, the nub of a dream, the part that sticks in the throat—in both, this often turns out to contain a power beyond its parts, and the release of this power can be cognate with a dramatic shift in consciousness. The key difference is in the precision of the dream with regard to our own particular blocks, wounds, and feelings.

Repeatedly in my dreams men would come for me. I'd be afraid of them: a scary chef with a large knife, a long-range desert truck driver whose eyes seemed to look right through me, a captain on a ship asking me to participate in a sea battle with nothing but a boat hook, and so on. Time after time, I would engage superficially with these men, then turn away, with a mix of fear and anger seething inside me. The therapy required me to sit with these feelings rather than seek to escape them. Bregman's work has a loose template for male dreamers, which is basically the journey of the prodigal son who surrenders his pride and returns, broken, to his true father. As he outlined the process, and as it unfolded in my own case, after a while I began to have dreams where I was a boy again. One night I dreamed that I was being rowed across a lake by my own father to a castle where a banquet was being prepared, and a man on a throne held out his hands to me. I sank to my knees in front of him, put my head in his lap, and began to sob. When I worked the dream, I was overcome by a wave of grief. For weeks after, I only had to put myself back in the dream to feel a profound sorrow washing over me. I'd weep as I hadn't in years. It felt profoundly healing, as if at last I was able to surrender myself to an infinite wound and find it somehow okay. At last I had opened to the trauma that had swamped me when I'd returned home at nineteen, which clearly dated from childhood losses and pains. I allowed them in. It was like rediscovering myself as an innocent, a child, a boy full of intense, fresh feeling; as a boy who loved his father and had come home.

In my outward life, I began to heal my long-broken relationship with my dad, fraught as it had been with divided loyalties. In my dream life, I frequently dreamed of myself as a child—riding on a man's shoulders, playing on swings with a man overseeing me, and so on. At the same time, I started to dream of being killed—by a mortar shell, by an assassin who shot me through the heart. I had dreams where I learned to breathe under water. All these, according to archetypal dreamwork, are indicators of "dying to the self" or becoming less attached to our ego-selves. I started to dream of myself as a girl. In one memorable dream I was standing before what I took to be a far-off range of hills, until it moved and I realized it was a giant reptile turning toward me. Instead of being scared, I made my stand and with complete courage cried out: "I come from God!" I didn't care what happened to me. I was functioning with a heart full of a power not my own. I also happened to be holding the very *kotsu*—or Zen teacher's stick—a master had recently given me.

Soon after that, I dreamed of being a crew member on an old sailing ship. A giant squid had been attacking us, and we hacked away at the last of its tentacles until it slid off and gave up the fight. Then the captain gave the order to sail west, and we headed off into the setting sun, toward some sublime new adventure. The feeling was glorious, like a long battle was over, a vital victory won.

The way I see it now, the transformative power of meditation has a profound ally in our dreams. They work the same defenses, in different but allied ways, battering our defended self until we give up and allow greater forces to work through us. Instead of knowing, we learn to not-know. Instead of being the hero of our own story, we become a servant, a helper, in a greater story. Archetypal dreamwork has helped me in my emotional and relational life. My marriage has been transformed into a field of love, of welcome challenges. Increasingly the archetypes, animus and anima, direct my actions rather than my own limited perspective. Likewise, my Zen teaching is not mine: I appeal to the masters to do it, and they do often seem to teach through me.

Perhaps those two early experiences, one of cosmic liberation, the other of existential despair, were less important in themselves than as gateways into two parallel journeys that in the end are only one journey:

of the soul's healing and awakening. We all know both rapture and despair: the first may drop us into a vast love, while the second asks us to face our own deep wounds. It is useless to ignore either. The whole soul must know both light and dark, suffering and awakening.

### IS THERE REALLY A DIFFERENCE?

If we truly embrace our existential suffering, as Buddha did, it turns out to be different from the horror we thought. What is the way to wholeness, to healing, to true helpfulness for ourselves and others? Surely it cannot ignore suffering, any more than it can ignore illumination by unnamable love.

Another way of looking at both koan and dream work is that our life is a story. We begin with one story of ourselves: our birth, childhood, youth, work, relationships. When we enter Zen training, we submit to another order of story in which we are lost beings struggling to find our way in a universe that makes no sense to us. We are asleep. Gradually we awaken from the dream of our life into another story, of liberation. Then we must awaken from that story, too, and forget all about it. Only then can we allow each moment to arise fully and freely.

Comparably in dream work we surrender to another order of narrative. We are no longer heroes in our stories. Instead we are errant creatures lost from our true home, gradually being coaxed back into the fold. Then the "story" of the old self is given up. We die to that self, primarily by opening to the feelings our dreams are asking us to experience. We pass through the keyhole of feeling, of woundedness, of trauma, into a new story, one we could never imagined, an epic in which we have only a bit part but find that a huge privilege.

Just as Zen opens up the possibility of dropping into timeless, spaceless reality, so dream work may open us to a vast wound. It's as if there's a psychological equivalent to spiritual experience, a place of infinite wounding in which we find infinite support. In the very heart of the feelings against which we protect ourselves, we find the love we seek, and our healing is found exactly where we'd last choose to look for it: right in the heart of the pain we thought we were trying to get away from.

# SETTLING THE MIND MEDITATION
## SUBJECTIVITY AND BEYOND

ADELINE VAN WANING

## INTRODUCTION

We may say that for Buddhism, on the one hand, and psychotherapy and depth psychology, on the other, the relief of suffering is the primary concern. While they may have different scopes, they share the view that the mind and our subjectivity are crucial sources of suffering. All three approaches have goals of lessening or, for Buddhism, ending suffering. It is in this context that I learned and practiced settling the mind in its natural state.

I invite you to join me in this practice, which I learned while taking part in a three-month meditation retreat combined with state-of-the-art scientific research. Participating in the Shamatha Project,

Adeline Van Waning, M.D., Ph.D., has worked as a psychiatrist, psychotherapist, and psychoanalyst at the University of Amsterdam, the Netherlands Psychoanalytical Institute, and Pharos—Health Services for Refugees. She has an M.A. in Buddhist studies and participated in the Shamatha Project, a three-month Buddhist meditation retreat combined with neuroscience research, in 2007. Her book on this expedition will be published in 2013 by Mantra Books. Her recent publications include "A Mindful Self and Beyond: Sharing in the Ongoing Dialogue of Buddhism and Psychoanalysis," in *Awakening and Insight: Buddhism and Psychotherapy East and West*, and "Naikan, a Buddhist Self-Reflective Approach: Psychoanalytic and Cultural reflections," in *Freud and the Far East—Psychoanalytic Perspectives on the People and Culture of China, Japan, and Korea*. She works in hospice care, offers meditation guidance, and paints.

which included cognitive and affective neuroscience and psychological research, nourished my ongoing commitment to exploring the mind and its wonders from various vantage points. As a psychiatrist and psychotherapist and a longtime practitioner of Buddhist meditation, I experience these varied perspectives as deeply enriching. During the retreat I felt at home with this practice of intimately exploring the mind, psyche, and subjectivity. It occurred to me that it would be a wonderful approach for psychotherapists, and possibly for clients in psychotherapy.

Here I offer a description of the instructions that I received from our meditation teacher that is very close to the actual experience, along with some ongoing personal and professional musings.

SETTLING THE MIND: A BRIEF CONTEXT

The Shamatha Project included two three-month retreats in 2007, during which a randomized, wait-list controlled study was conducted. "Meditate to advance science—be part of this groundbreaking neuroscience research project exploring the relationship between meditation and well-being" was the advertisement for the project— supported by His Holiness the Dalai Lama—that brought me to the United States from my home in Holland.

"Shamatha" stands for concentration-calm meditation. Coleaders for the ongoing project are B. Alan Wallace, Ph.D., contemplative director and meditation teacher, and Clifford Saron, Ph.D., scientific director and neuroscientist.[1] Their team hypothesized that three months of shamatha training, combined with cultivation of the Four Qualities of the Heart (loving kindness, compassion, empathetic joy, and equanimity), would result in improved attentional performance as well as greater compassion, security, and ability to regulate negative emotions.

The attention practices had as their focus various aspects of breathing, the mind, and awareness. Here I will just address the main mind practice: settling the mind in its natural state. In the Tibetan Buddhist view, a global distinction may be made in three forms of practice: concentration-calm practices (*śamatha* or *shamatha*), insight practices (*vipassanā* or *vipashyana*), and what are called essential practices, *mahāmudrā* and Dzogchen. Shamatha practices are foundational for insight and essential practices. While settling the mind in its natural state is not an insight practice in the Buddhist sense, it nevertheless allows many psychological insights to come to mind. Considered to be an important concentration practice in the essential traditions, settling the mind in its natural state offers a way of relating to the mind and prepares the mind for more extensive insight practices.

SETTLING THE MIND IN ITS NATURAL STATE—GUIDED MEDITATION I

Here are a few general shamatha notions as explained by Alan Wallace. *Mindfulness,* while often used in contemporary Western context to refer to moment-to-moment nonjudgmental awareness, in this Tibetan tradition stands for attending continuously to a familiar object without forgetfulness or distraction. The object of mindfulness is what you choose to focus your attention on, for example, the breath, a mental image, or the space of mind. An important aspect in this approach is *meta-awareness*: while the main force of attention is directed to the meditation object, this needs to be supported with the faculty of awareness which allows for the control of attention, enabling you to swiftly note when the mind has fallen into either excitation or laxity and to make the necessary adjustments. The instruction is to meditate without distraction or grasping.

Following is an example of the way Alan Wallace, after some introduction by way of the breath, guided the meditation on the mind during the project retreat.[2] This practice became one of my favorites during the retreat, and I've continued doing it regularly since then.

> Let us settle the mind in its natural state.
>
> In this practice the object of mindfulness is the space of the mind and whatever arises in it.
>
> In this practice, we let the eyes be at least partially open and the gaze resting vacantly in the space in front of you. We do not focus on any visual object, any shape or color, just rest the gaze vacantly . . . And now, direct the full force of your mindfulness to the space of mental events: events or contents of experience that cannot be detected with any of the five physical senses or any of the instruments of technology, the space in which discursive thoughts arise, mental chitchat, mental images, memories, fantasies, desires and emotions, all manner of mental events . . .

Now quietly observe whatever next arises within this field, this space of the mind, be it another discursive thought, perhaps a mental image, and whatever arises, just let it be as you attend to it with discerning mindfulness, in no way trying to reorder or modify the contents of the mind.

The space of the mind doesn't have any particular location in front or behind, down, above or below. It is simply a domain of experience, the one that remains after excluding visual, hearing, smelling, tasting, and touching.

The essence of this practice is to attend to the space of the mind and its contents without distraction and without grasping. Distraction occurs when we are carried away by a thought, into the past, imaginary future, or into thoughts about the present, or to the referent of the thought.

Grasping occurs whenever we latch onto mental events as "I" or "mine," identifying with that which arises or responding liking this, disliking that. Attend to it for what it is—an event arising in the space of the mind, with no owner, no controller. Having no preference also includes not having a preference for the thoughts to dissipate and dissolve back into the space of awareness. Be as indifferent as space itself, nonreactively attending toward whatever arises, illuminating its nature without interference.

Whatever arises, be it pleasant or unpleasant, wholesome or unwholesome, long or short, subtle or coarse, let it be and observe the nature of whatever arises in the mind with discerning mindfulness . . .

Bring the full force of your mindfulness, the focus, the attention, to the domain of experience that is purely mental in nature, selecting out all the appearances that arise to the physical senses, allowing them to arise, of course, we have no other option, but not paying attention, not deliberately focusing on, not taking an interest in any of the five physical sense fields.

In many cases you may be aware of the thought, the image, certainly the emotion, only after it's arisen; it may have gone on for some seconds before you're aware of it. But as soon as you become aware of it, simply direct your mindfulness there, as you release the grasping. Just let the thought, image, whatever it may be, just let it arise with as little entanglement as possible . . .

As soon as you know that your mind has been caught up in excitation, distraction, or agitation, release not the thought but your grasping onto it, and relax more deeply while letting the thought be, without banishing it. Unlike other shamatha practices, here we do not banish or let go of the thought. We do not even prefer for there to be fewer thoughts. Instead, we simply release the grasping onto the thought and observe whatever thoughts arise in the mind with unwavering mindfulness.

Exercise stability and wakefulness as qualities of the subjective attention, not of the objective content of the mind—that comes and goes, is sometimes very chaotic; you exercise the instrument of focused attention . . .

The following topics frequently arose as questions.

Why do we keep the eyes open with a gaze? Alan explained that the artificial barrier between "inner" and "outer" begins to dissolve in this way. In the beginning I found this was not easy, but it was supportive to keep the field of vision clear of moving objects. Some people have problems "finding" the space of the mind. Alan advised us to deliberately generate a discursive thought—for example, "this is the mind"—and then slowly and deliberately generate this mental sentence, syllable by syllable. While doing so, you direct full attention to this mental event. As soon as that thought has vanished, back into the space of the mind, fix your attention on where it was and then you have found the domain. Certainly in the beginning, my subjective awareness was mainly with the objective phenomena arising in the space of the mind, and sometimes I was completely identified with thought trains and persisting memories. As mindfulness gradually became more stable, I grew more familiar with the space and what arises there, in an observing and witnessing way.

In the course of practicing settling the mind, it becomes quite clear that habitual thinking, grasping, daydreaming are quite different from what we may see as the bare activity of the mental sense. The last, referred to as the sixth sense in Buddhism, is a "clean" mental cognizing, or discerning, that is stripped from all grasping and identifications around it.

### THE PRACTICE IN RELATION TO PSYCHOTHERAPEUTIC BENEFITS

Some results of the discerning, nongrasping activity in settling the
mind are described by Wallace in the following way:

> What happens here is a kind of luminously clear, discerning,
> free association of thoughts, mental images, memories, desires,
> fantasies, and emotions. You are plumbing the depths of your
> own mind, undistracted by external diversions. Once-hidden
> phenomena are unmasked through the lack of suppression of
> whatever comes up. This is *potentially an extraordinarily deep
> kind of therapy* . . . This is the key to letting the knots of the
> psyche unravel themselves as the extraordinary healing
> capacity of the mind reveals itself. This is the *path to deep
> sanity*. [italics added][3]

For me, the practice of neither grasping at thoughts nor banishing them
brings greater familiarity with mind and its contents. The practice also
brings a sense of "melting"—at first, this felt like softening of old
neurotic knots, but then gradually also a softening of the habitual
familiar sense of a seemingly separate-self. Clearing this "path to deep
sanity"—as Wallace calls it—naturally loosens our identification with
a sense of separate self (the idea of being an independent, inherent
self) and may provoke fear and anxiety. Such a loosening is described
in the texts, and I experienced a deepening in this gradual process
during the three-month retreat. For example, a sense of anger about
some remark that was made earlier that day might lead to a reactive
grasping for an identity that could be felt as some energy shift, a
contraction in my body-mind. Regarding this seeming "identity
formation," Jack Engler quotes the psychoanalyst Herbert Fingarette:
"It is conflict or anxiety that turns us back to check up on and reassure
ourselves, and in so doing literally brings a 'self' into being as a structure
separate from its experience."[4]

The beauty is that with numerous repetitions of this practice of
concentration-calm and witnessing emotional states, traits can evolve.
Surprisingly, I found that *resilience* can be much strengthened with the
practice of settling the mind. Moving through turbulence with intense
emotions such as anger or joy in a process that desensitizes anxiety, I
was able to train my capacity to be with the turbulence for now and
for the future. Sustaining such a matter-of-fact capacity increases our
ease and lightness in all activities.

To my feeling, with this practice the self-healing and re-owning of hidden materials can be quite extensive. However, the gentle unraveling of self-healing may not be enough for melting and dissolving very strong self-reinforcing defensive knots, fixations, and shadows—the dark rejected parts in the psyche. I believe that tenaciously repeating patterns of grasping show where it might be advisable to do more robust therapeutic work with a supportive "outer" witness in an intersubjective framework. In such circumstances, a psychotherapist may be consulted for sharing additional ways of seeing and understanding the origins of the need for hiding and the structural developmental history of the person. Such therapeutic practices support the reclaiming of hidden aspects of the psyche.

### A Larger View: The Union of Stillness and Motion—Guided Meditation II

The following are instructions for a second practice in settling the mind in its natural state. It is assumed that the person has done the first practice for some time and has acquired some skill in it. This second practice includes going beyond what is usually recognized in Western psychology as the typical sense of an individual and separate self. Here is a summary of some guidance for this practice, which is called the union of stillness and motion:

> After you have grown familiar with observing mental images and thoughts . . . continue observing the space of your mind and anything that arises within it. This mental space is not located in any specific physical region, and it *doesn't have a center, a periphery, a size, or borders.* When you begin to observe thoughts and images, you may find that they disappear as soon as you notice them. Be patient and relax more deeply. Then you will begin to discover a place of stillness within the motion of your mind . . . .
>
> The mind is constantly in motion, but in the midst of the movements of thoughts and images *there is a still space of awareness* in which you can rest in the present moment, without being jerked around through space and time by the contents of your mind. This is the union of stillness and motion. Whatever events arise in your mind—be they pleasant or unpleasant, gentle or harsh, good or bad, long or short—just let them be . . . .

> You may begin to detect very subtle mental events that had
> previously escaped your notice. Because they are so subtle, they
> slip under the radar of ordinary consciousness . . . Some may
> persist for seconds at a time, barely crossing the threshold of
> consciousness because of their subtlety; others may flit across the
> space of your mind for only a fraction of a second. As your
> mindfulness becomes more and more continuous, you may detect
> these micro-events for the first time . . . .
>
> Like reflections in a mirror, these thoughts and images have no
> power of their own to harm you or to help you. They are as
> insubstantial as mirages and rainbows, yet they have their own
> reality, as they causally interact among themselves and with your
> body. As you discover the luminous still space of awareness in
> which the movements of the mind occur, you will begin to
> discover *an inner freedom and place of rest* even when the storms of
> turbulent emotions and desires sweep through this inner domain.[5]

We are invited here to become more familiar with the motion, the
events, the movements of the mind and the stillness of the space of
mind or awareness. This space is the vantage point of what is referred
to as "storehouse or substrate consciousness." It has no center and
no periphery. While there are some commonalities of this notion
with the collective unconscious in the Jungian view, there are also
crucial differences.[6]

In the end, the union of stillness and motion refers to finding
increasing depth and width in one's access to various levels of awareness
and, on a deeper level, a union in stillness and motion. As Thrangu
Rinpoche, a contemporary Tibetan teacher says: "On the conventional
level, mind and thoughts appear to be different." However, in the
context of deep meditative experience, he continues: "From this point
of view thoughts are co-emergent—there is no difference between
thoughts and mind."[7] Observing but not entering into thoughts and
conditioned association chains releases familiar identifications and
clarifies the realization of no separate self, only an impermanent and
ever-changing flux of perceptions and reactions, thoughts and emotions,
hopes and fears, habits and motivations, projected onto the external
world. While these practices require unlearning and de-conditioning
operations that are tremendously challenging, they are supported by

gradual, subtle confirmation in a sense of greater ease and relaxation, with greater presence and authenticity in the body-mind.

The following are therapeutic and existential benefits that, in my view, may directly arise from practicing settling the mind:

1. Increasing concentration-calm
2. More detailed pattern recognition in mental contents, including on a deeper nondiscursive level
3. Melting of neurotic knots in self-healing
4. Increasing sense of focus and resilience in addressing larger neurotic themes—possibly together with a therapist
5. Some melting in the sense of separate self with a sense of ease and lightness spilling over to daily life

Settling the mind has a special contribution to daily life "off the cushion": increasing our ability for observing and witnessing thought and emotion while not grasping and behaving reactively will bear fruit in many ways in our relationships and work. And in the case of the second practice, as we become more skillful in it, we move from being identified with self, to being and living Self in a wider, transpersonal context; Self that transcends and includes self.

As Radmila Moacanin says in describing the Jungian approach: the process of individuation leads progressively further away from the self to the Self, "from unconscious to conscious, from the personal to the transpersonal, the holy, the realization that the macrocosm is being mirrored in the microcosm of the human psyche."[8]

When I use the term *self* in lower case, I am referring to the representation of a function of coherence, continuity, agency, and relationship that allows us to perceive ourselves as a single, integrated, subjective embodiment. The capitalized *Self* refers to the quintessential archetype of self-realization of consciousness unified with the formless source.

## CONNECTIONS

Alan Wallace teaches settling the mind in ways derived from various teachers through the ages, including Lerab Lingpa and Düdjom Lingpa, both great meditation masters who lived in nineteenth-century Tibet. I am struck by the parallels between what they have described and what was recommended by Jung and Freud.

Jung emphasizes the necessity of noninterference: "The art of letting things happen, action through inaction, letting go of oneself . . . became for me the key that opens the door to the way. We must be able to let things happen in the psyche."[9] And Freud reminds us: "Act as though . . . you were a traveller sitting next to the window of a railway carriage and describing to someone inside the carriage the changing views which you see outside."[10] Settling the mind provides particular methods for training ourselves in nonjudgmental awareness, which supports the loosening of reactive and ingrained intra- and interpersonal patterns. Nondistraction and nongrasping, with nonidentification with thoughts, brings a natural peace of mind and, as an outflow, a natural ability to help others more skillfully.

Settling the mind, as a practice, can be of great support and enrichment to all psychotherapists and analysts. And it may also be recommendable for certain therapeutic clients. This meditation adds to conventional therapy a way to go beyond fixed separate-self identifications that releases us from much deep suffering.

### NOTES

1. B. Alan Wallace, Ph.D., is a Tibetan Buddhist meditation teacher and author. Clifford Saron, Ph.D., is a neuroscientist at the University of California, Davis. More information on the Shamatha Project—including confirming and surprising outcomes—can be found at http://www.sbinstitute.com/Shamatha_Project and http://mindbrain.ucdavis.edu/labs/Saron/shamatha-project. See also Adeline Van Waning, "Inside the Shamatha Project," *Buddhadharma: The Practitioner's Quarterly* (Summer 2011), pp. 38–45; http://db.tt/0BZqJjj4.

2. Transcribed from a recording made September 7, 2007, of Alan Wallace conducting the meditation, settling the mind in its natural state, during the Shamatha Project.

3. Alan Wallace, *The Attention Revolution—Unlocking the Power of the Focused Mind* (Somerville, MA: Wisdom Publications, 2006), p. 102.

4. Jack Engler, "Being Somebody and Being Nobody: A Re-examination of the Understanding of Self in Psychoanalysis and Buddhism," in *Psychoanalysis and Buddhism*, ed. Jeremy D. Safran (Somerville, MA: Wisdom Publications, 2003), pp. 62–63.

5. From "The Union of Stillness and Motion," chapter 7, in Alan Wallace, *Mind in the Balance: Meditation in Science, Buddhism, and Christianity* (New York: Columbia University Press, 2009), pp. 48–51; italics added.

6. Buddhist views of the substrate consciousness are in terms of an individual stream of consciousness, and this stream flows from one lifetime into the next.

7. Khenchen Thrangu Rinpoche, *Essentials of Mahamudra: Looking Directly at the Mind* (Somerville, MA: Wisdom Publications, 2004), p. 158.

8. Radmila Moacanin, *Jung's Psychology and Tibetan Buddhism* (Boston: Wisdom Publications, 1986), p. 65.

9. Carl G. Jung, from "Commentary on the Secret of the Golden Flower," quoted in Moacanin, *Jung's Psychology and Tibetan Buddhism*, p. 43.

10. Sigmund Freud, "On Beginning the Treatment (Further Recommendations on the Technique of Psychoanalysis)," vol. 12, *Standard Edition of the Complete Psychological Works of Sigmund Freud*, ed. and trans. James Strachey (London: Hogarth Press, 1913; reprinted 1958), p. 135.

# ON BEING A ZEN PSYCHOANALYST
## THE UNION OF PRESENCE, MEANING, AND INTIMACY

JEFFREY B. RUBIN

Both psychoanalysis and Zen are concerned with alleviating suffering and illuminating human identity. Each has a "treatment plan" as well as a diagnosis of what truly afflicts us. And both can help us lessen anguish through clarity and equanimity while exploring what it means to be fully human and experiencing greater intimacy and wisdom. Increasingly, practitioners of each are using—even blending—insights and practices from both, leading to mutual enrichment.[1]

Being a Zen psychoanalyst, just like working with a Zen koan, has two aspects: realization and actualization. We need to understand and explain the Zen koans, and then practice and embody them. In this paper I will show how I have practiced and embodied Zen and psychoanalysis. I will begin with some introductory remarks about Zen.

Jeffrey B. Rubin, Ph.D., is a practicing psychotherapist and teacher of meditation in New York City and Bedford Hills, New York. Considered one of the leading integrators of the Western psychotherapeutic and Eastern meditative traditions, he is the creator of meditative psychotherapy. Rubin is the author of *Meditative Psychotherapy, The Art of Flourishing, Psychotherapy and Buddhism, The Good Life,* and *A Psychoanalysis for Our Time.* He has taught at various universities, psychoanalytic institutes, and Buddhist and yoga centers. His pioneering approach to psychotherapy and Buddhism has been featured in the *New York Times Magazine.* His website is drjeffreyrubin.com.

"You know, you're a Zen guy," my patient, who was a Zen master, said to me.

Around the same time, a snarky, middle-aged man asked me, "What *is* Zen?" as I was leaving the gym.

"It began many centuries ago in China," I said, in a remarkably un-Zen-like response.

"Gimme the short version," he shot back.

"Did you have coffee this morning?" I asked.

"Yeah." He raised his Styrofoam cup.

"Did you really taste it, or were you a million miles away?"

"I really tasted it."

"That's Zen," I said.

"Okay, I can go with that."

"Zen is teaching adults what comes naturally to children," I added as I walked past him.

The process of growing up and becoming an adult—learning a language, categorizing the world around us, and mastering the rules and roles that make up our culture—alienates us from ourselves and from a natural, spontaneous, and authentic way of being. We lose our imaginative, freewheeling childhood spirit in our quest to become practical, realistic, and competent adults who can earn money, succeed at work, find a mate, and raise a family.[2]

Zen meditation reopens our latent capacity for freshness of perception, wonder, and delight. Not only do we become more open and receptive to the world, we are capable of bearing witness to a greater range of human experience. This is, in and of itself, wonderfully therapeutic.

A student met with a venerable Zen teacher who told him he was riddled with depression and fear. The rōshi recommended Zen therapy. "When you completely listen to the sound of the birds, where is your depression?" the rōshi asked. "When you chop vegetables, where is your fear?" To a Western-trained psychotherapist this is intriguing, if unusual, advice. Most of the time we sleepwalk through our days—lost in ruminative thoughts, pointless worries, and countless pseudo-problems. Meanwhile, we suffer unnecessarily and miss so much. The lives of psychotherapists as well as clients would be greatly enhanced if they spent more time directly engaging their experiences. Fears about the future and regrets from the past would both lessen if we followed the rōshi's advice.

Thinking about Zen therapy left me with several questions: Is merging with whatever we encounter enough? Is it ever too narrow an approach? Is there what Jung would call a shadow side to it?

Even those trained in meditation spend an inordinate amount of time inside their heads, disconnected from life, worrying about what hasn't happened and regretting what has. Even extraordinary experiences in meditation do not make us immune to loss and conflict. Emotions are feedback about what we value and struggle with. If we could merge with the song of the birds or the act of cutting veggies without interruption, it could interfere with learning what our emotions are communicating. Anger can signal hurt; jealousy tells us what we want more of in our lives. Healing our wounds and conflicts lies in integrating our emotions, which entails understanding them, not simply merging with them.[3]

When Cindy, a therapist in training with a severe trauma history, told her previous therapist, who was a Buddhist, about her extreme suffering, he asked: "Where is the self who is suffering?" She was stumped. And not only didn't her suffering diminish, her shame increased. She only got better when we carefully explored and illuminated her depression and fear and understood how they interacted with her identity and roles.

One way of salvaging the rōshi's insights about Zen therapy is to integrate them with two hallmarks of psychoanalysis, namely, a search for meaning and a focus on relationality. While Buddhism neglects meaning, psychoanalysts devote a great deal of attention to illuminating the meaning of the symptoms and symbols patients bring to treatment. Although Zen can be highly therapeutic, what the rōshi recommended as Zen therapy is not truly therapy unless it focuses on meaning, as well as merging with and becoming deeply connected to what we encounter.

One of Freud's towering insights was that people grow ill—and suffer from—experiences that they don't understand. "Find out about the parent they don't talk about, not the one they do," a Freudian supervisor of mine once aptly noted. While humans have an infinite capacity for self-deception, we also have a remarkable ability to communicate what troubles and haunts us by means of symbols, dreams, and symptoms. These offer clues—breadcrumbs leading to the source and current manifestation of our problems. And a therapeutic relationship, suffused with empathy, compassion, and understanding, provides an unsurpassed vehicle for working through a person's difficulties in living and embodying new ways of being.

To understand these clues we have to illuminate their symbolic meaning, which occurs on various levels at once. This is one of the great therapeutic discoveries.

### All Psychiatrists Are Assholes

They sat on my couch: a brilliant and cantankerous thirteen-year-old boy and his mother, a lawyer. Actually, she sat and he fidgeted and sank down, at one point putting his head on her lap. She was at her wit's end: her husband had killed himself the year before, and her son was desolate and depressed to the point of being suicidal. She did most of the talking, filling in the horrific details of the tragedy she and her son had endured in the past year. They had both lost the person most important to them, a man with a commanding personality and titanic intellect, who alternately challenged and fiercely loved his son. The boy said very little. He was busy checking me out and gauging whether I could be trusted. He had spent the previous year seeing a variety of psychiatrists and psychologists, none of whom had connected with him.

As I ended the session, I caught a fleeting glimpse of the statue of the Buddha on the windowsill of my office, his face eclipsed by a curtain, obscuring his beatific smile. I got up from my chair and stood near the door. My prospective patient lumbered toward me, his mother at his flank.

"All psychiatrists are assholes," he informed me.

"There are two problems with your statement," I said. "One, I am a psychoanalyst, not a psychiatrist. Two, given your supposed intelligence, why did it take you so long to figure out my limitations?"

"I'm going to poison my mother," the boy replied.

"Thank you," I said.

"You can't say thank you, you're a shrink," he responded, momentarily flustered, trying for damage control.

"Well, *you've* given *me* a new strategy I can employ against stubborn teenage boys," I told him.

The tiny half smile on the right side of his mouth showed me I'd hit home.

I didn't consciously plan my response. When the boy challenged me at the door my mind was free of preconceptions, receptive to his tone of voice and the humor—and vulnerability—underneath his apparent hostility. It can be scary to be without a map or a compass, a particular theory or set response to draw on. My experience over the years has cultivated a deep faith in the capacity of patients to creatively communicate what they feel and need but cannot always say. My capacity to hear was infinitely increased when I put aside both what I thought I knew and any preconceived ideas about how therapy should proceed. And that provided access to a state of mind that Japanese artists, meditators, and martial artists call *mushin*, or no-mindedness, what D. T. Suzuki described as awareness-without-self-consciousness.[4]

## Discovering Meaning

It is infinitely harder to merge with a painful emotion than with the song of the birds, but the process is the same. What I call training meditation-in-action offers a means of practicing this in stages. First we can open to sights and sounds that are either pleasing or neutral by attempting to be one with them and savor them. This develops concentration and equanimity, which can serve as a foundation to merge with pleasant or neutral physical sensations. Once that is manageable—whether it takes minutes or days, weeks or months—the meditator can practice becoming one with more challenging physical sensations. Eventually we can merge with physical pain. We can then practice merging with pleasant or mildly afflictive emotions (such as disappointment or slight anxiety). Then we can tackle slightly more challenging emotions. Eventually we can practice merging with anger, guilt, and fear.

Discovering meaning is the second aspect of Zen psychoanalysis. Meaning can be confusing because it is sometimes disguised and can't be found on the surface. Decoding is often necessary.

We never know the meaning of something in advance. "What is the meaning of such [flying] dreams?" asked Freud. "It is impossible to give a general reply. As we shall hear, they mean something different in every instance."[5]

Meaning is arrived at, as Freud recognized, not by translating what you are examining into what you already know or assume, but by eliciting the person's unique associations or reactions. Otherwise you interpret "into" the experience what cannot be interpreted "from" it. We find meaning by paying attention to and being one with the cause and the function (or purpose) of a thought, feeling, or action, which includes the emergent potentials it embodies. Listening deeply on two levels or channels at once—conscious and unconscious—is indispensable. Meditation training neglects the latter.[6]

Sometimes meaning emerges directly and automatically when we are truly one with what we are experiencing—like my playful encounter with the bereaved teenager. Zen calls this *prajna* wisdom or intuition. At other times, being in the moment is not enough to determine meaning, and one needs to step back from direct contact with a person or emotion and reflect on it—what I call reflective intimacy. What did my teenaged patient mean when he said, "All psychiatrists are assholes," and why did he say it? On the surface his remark might seem angry and hostile, a direct attack. He just met me, and he was making a blanket and provocative statement that I was a jerk. But why? I thought he was asking several questions: How free and safe is it here for him to be himself? Could I deal with his rage and impotent confusion? Would I retaliate if he expressed hostility?

But there was even more. Was he pushing me away because he was afraid of getting close, relying on me and then being abandoned like his father had left him? Or had he become like his father, a highly critical person who was never satisfied with anything? Was he treating me the way he had been treated? Or was he feeling safe enough to say that psychiatrists, as well as mothers and fathers, had profoundly let him down?

As I listened to my young patient over time, I heard a soul in trouble, a person who had been devastated, and perhaps more important, had not been encouraged to mourn his loss. He was literally imploding under the house arrest inadvertently imposed by his grieving mother, who was facing her own personal nightmare and didn't have the energy to handle his rage and torment. He felt poisoned by both his father's death and his mother's failure to help him face it. He longed for an opportunity to have his pain witnessed and validated. So when he challenged me, I heard it as an expression of how he felt and as a test—was it safe enough to be real? I sensed he needed me to meet his onslaught without flinching. I could have asked him if he was angry or betrayed or afraid, but I believed he needed actions rather than words to know it was safe to trust me and be himself.

When we talked about that first session a decade later, he said: "My statement about psychiatrists was my way of letting you know that I wouldn't defer to you because of age or stature," he said. "My statement about my mother conveyed that therapy won't fix anything, you don't have control and I'm angry."

In retrospect, I'm glad I said "Thank you" when he said he was going to poison his mother. I was relieved that he felt safe enough to challenge me and be aggressive and authentic. Meeting his challenge seemed crucial to launching the therapy. Exploring his wish to poison his mother ("Why do you think you said that?") or being subtly shocked or disturbed by it would have conveyed, I suspect, that I couldn't handle his emotions. It would have doomed the therapy from the start. My humor communicated to him that I had the endurance to handle him *and* that I liked him.

I learned recently that my patient, now in his late twenties, has graduated from one of the best law schools in the world and has a job at an esteemed law firm. He was following his passion, drawing on his unique strengths, and embodying his talents and skills.

### Zen and Relationships

My work with Cindy, the therapist in training with a severe trauma history mentioned at the beginning of this paper, elucidates the third aspect of being a Zen psychoanalyst—the importance of a self-reflective, empathic, and playful human relationship. Psychoanalysis enriches Zen with its provision of a collaborative relationship designed to validate the client's experience and provide opportunities for new forms of relatedness and self-transformation.

In the midst of our work, after a deep connection was established and many traumatic memories had emerged, Cindy indicated that she felt worse—and stuck. Frozen physical energy, terror, and mental lethargy had become constant companions. As we explored her emotions, various meanings emerged—especially the way she felt in danger of being abandoned and re-traumatized by me. She seemed relieved but still somewhat stymied. I eventually wondered if the closeness of our relationship was making her feel worse because if someone she liked and respected valued her, then maybe she wasn't loathsome, which made her feel even more betrayed by the people who hadn't protected her from past abuse.

As I reflected on her predicament, Kyogen's "Man up in a Tree" koan, one that I had encountered in my own training to be a Zen teacher, came to mind.[7] A man who is up in a tree, hanging from a branch by his mouth, is asked by a man under the tree, "What is the meaning of Bodhidharma's coming from the west?" The man hanging by his mouth is in a desperate predicament. He will fail if he doesn't say something, and he will drop to his death if he does. We often find ourselves in a related dilemma in therapy and in our lives when we must respond to something when we seemingly can't—no good options seem available, and we don't know what to do.

My client, like all of us, couldn't cure herself alone. She needed someone to witness and validate her trauma and pain, yet trusting—and relying on—other people was terrifying and revealing her abuse was forbidden by her abusers. They'd threatened to kill her if she did. I knew that she was an imaginative therapist and a talented artist who regularly used art—and Jung's technique of active imagination, or artistically exploring symbolic imagery in dreams—to access and examine her emotions.[8] Knowing that speaking about how she was traumatized was itself traumatic, I suggested a "life koan" for her: "How can you communicate what you need to with me *without* talking about it?"

"I'll bring in artwork on Friday," she said with a noticeable sigh of relief.

That Friday she brought in a brightly colored mask with a closed mouth and a picture of a gun pointing toward a person. She looked terrified and lost.

"What would happen if you punctured the mask?" I asked.

She took out a pen, punctured the sealed mouth, and began speaking about how she'd been traumatized by a religious cult her parents sent her to and forbidden to speak about it. She also revealed new aspects of her trauma and her self-silencing. "It was freeing to do that," she said. "I felt trapped and couldn't speak. Without you asking me that question I couldn't have done it."

Since that time she has spoken more freely and deeply about her traumas. She is slowly healing. She has also found her voice in her psychoanalytic classes and is noticeably more engaged in treatment.

These vignettes illustrate the three main elements of being a Zen psychoanalyst: the union of intimacy, meaning, and relationality. Regarding intimacy, wholehearted and unself-conscious engagement with what we experience can lead to emotional closeness and unpredictable encounters, both inside and outside therapy. Zen practice—with its emphasis on unqualified and unself-conscious immersion in whatever we encounter—can greatly enrich our capacities as a person or a therapist.

Psychoanalytic attention to unconscious communication and meaning—the second facet of Zen psychoanalysis—expands the intimacy that meditation fosters. After establishing good therapeutic relationships with patients, I need to understand the unconscious meanings of their words and actions.

The third and final aspect of being a Zen analyst is a special relationship (and environment) designed to illuminate and transform one's history. Psychoanalysis not only elucidates the interpersonal roots of adult afflictions, it offers a relationship and experience that is a vehicle for transformation in the present.

If psychoanalysis and Zen can be judiciously integrated, we might have a civilization with greater meaning and less discontent.[9]

## NOTES

1. See J. B. Rubin, *Psychotherapy and Buddhism: Toward an Integration* (New York: Plenum, 1996); B. Magid, *Ordinary Mind: Exploring the Common Ground of Zen and Psychotherapy* (Boston: Wisdom Publications, 2002); and P. Young-Eisendrath, "Transference and Transformation in Buddhism and Psychoanalysis," in *Psychoanalysis and Buddhism: An Unfolding Dialogue*, ed. Jeremy Safran (Boston: Wisdom Publications, 2003), pp. 301–318.

2. J. B. Rubin, *The Art of Flourishing: A New East-West Approach to Staying Sane and Finding Love in an Insane World* (New York: Crown, 2011).

3. *Ibid.*

4. D. T. Suzuki, *Zen and Japanese Culture* (Princeton, NJ: Princeton University Press, 1971).

5. S. Freud, *The Interpretation of Dreams*, vols. 4 and 5, *Standard Edition of the Complete Psychological Works of Sigmund Freud*, ed. and trans. James Strachey (London: Hogarth Press, 1900), pp. 392–393.

6. J. B. Rubin, "Deepening Psychoanalytic Listening: The Marriage of Buddha and Freud," *American Journal of Psychoanalysis* 69 (2009): 93–105.

7. K. Sekida, *The Gateless Gate* (Boston: Shambhala, 2005), pp. 38–41.

8. On active imagination, see C. G. Jung, *Memories, Dreams, Reflections* (New York: Random House, 1961); and C. G. Jung, *The Red Book*, ed. Sonu Shamdasani (New York: Norton, 2009).

9. I am grateful to Lou Mitsunen Nordstrom, Polly Young-Eisendrath, and Siobhan Drummond, whose thoughtful feedback enriched this paper.

# Unconscious and Conscious Meet Self and self
## Depth Psychology and Zen Meditation

GRACE JILL SCHIRESON

There are several ways to explore the relationship between Zen meditation and depth psychology. First, what common ground do they explore? Second, what are their common aims? Third how do they accomplish their aims? Depth psychology and Zen meditation both explore a patient's or practitioner's conversation between the conscious and unconscious aspects of mind. Both methods rely on an intermediary to facilitate the relationship between conscious and unconscious, both methods unfold according to the individual's unique needs, and both methods aim to free a person of neurotic or habitually conditioned unwholesome behaviors through the conversation between conscious and unconscious.

Grace Schireson is a Zen abbess, president of Shogaku Zen Institute (a Zen teachers' training seminary), and a clinical psychologist. She received her doctorate at the Wright Institute in Berkeley, California. She received Dharma Transmission from Sojun Mel Weitsman Roshi of the Suzuki Roshi Zen lineage. The late Fukushima Keido Roshi of Tofukuji Monastery, Kyoto, asked her to teach the koan she studied with him during her practice there. She leads two practice centers and a retreat center under the Central Valley Zen Foundation. She is the author of *Zen Women: Beyond Tea Ladies, Iron Maidens and Macho Masters* (2009) and has published articles in *Shambhala Sun*, *Buddhadharma*, and *Tricycle* magazines. She has also been anthologized in *The Book of Mu*, *Receiving the Marrow*, and *The Hidden Lamp*. She lives with her husband at her Zen retreat center, Empty Nest Zendo, in North Fork, California.

This paper will briefly outline three similarities between depth psychology and Zen meditation and then focus specifically on three stages of Zen meditation that offer personal transformation in order to free a practitioner from habitually conditioned reactivity and related suffering.

### THREE SIMILARITIES

In depth psychology patient and therapist bring to the surface and explore unseen forces between conscious and unconscious understanding in an effort to transform human suffering and provide deeper meaning. C. G. Jung remarked:

> Consciousness, no matter how extensive it may be, must always remain the smaller circle within the greater circle of the unconscious, an island surrounded by the sea; and like the sea itself, the unconscious yields an endless and self-replenishing abundance of creatures, a wealth beyond our fathoming.[1]

In Zen, one also increases conscious access to unconscious material. Rather than relying on the analytical training and skills of a therapist, Zen meditation provides a practitioner direct experience of the hidden Self or the "ocean of Buddhahood" within which we exist.[2] As twentieth-century Zen teacher Uchiyama says,

> The spirit enmeshed in the Buddha's teaching refuses to offer a god in exchange for freedom from anxiety. Instead, freedom from anxiety can only be found at that point where the Self naturally settles upon itself. When doing *zazen* [meditation] we practice ceasing to project some goal separate from the Self. Instead we learn to live out completely the Self which settles upon itself.[3]

Meditating, we have personal and intimate access to this Self, the vast formless awareness. This Self is like the ocean or the unconscious surrounding the conscious personal self. One's individual self is revealed, known, and may be transformed through contact with this universal awareness.

The second shared ground is that each practitioner explores the relationship between conscious and unconscious at his/her own unique pace. Jung asserted that each patient required his or her own individual course of therapy. Jung was not validating or proving a theory through treatment. He emphasized, rather, how trusting attention allowed a patient to improve.

> [The patient] then made a devastatingly frank confession, which showed me the reasons for the peculiar course our treatment had followed. The original shock had been such that he could not face it alone. It needed the two of us, and that was the therapeutic task, not the fulfillment of theoretical presuppositions.[4]

From Jung's description of treatment, we learn that the therapist's steady, focused attention is essential in treating a patient's psychological problem. This process unfolds without rigid reference to a specific theory. The patient and the therapist together uncover the protective layers that have encapsulated the conflict, gently allowing unconscious subterranean issues to surface. In depth psychology, patient and therapist together create space for exploring unknown aspects of self in relationship. This process results in transformation through self-knowledge. In Zen, the practitioner exposes his mind, issues, and trauma to the meditative process rather than to another person.

The Buddha stated, "Be a lamp unto yourself," offering self-knowledge as the responsibility of each individual. Buddha taught self-illumination rather than dependence on a particular doctrine. The Buddha fully endorses Jung's words: theory alone will not heal a person; each person needs to unfold as himself or herself at a personal pace. Each has the ability to experience insight, to study the personal self without following a specific theoretical plan. The deeper layers of self-construction are uniquely revealed and transformed in the relationship between the practitioner's mind and the larger space of meditative awareness.

As expressed by Zen founder Eihei Dōgen (1200–1253): "To study the Buddha Way is to study the self."[5] Buddhist practice is self-study, an intimate relationship between meditator and meditative awareness. Like depth psychology, the Zen path to freedom requires that aspects of personal self must become more fully known. A practitioner becomes free from the limitations of self through self-study and self-awareness in meditation. Dōgen asserted that one must start right where she or he is and patiently study the self. Similar to depth psychotherapy, one starts by studying the personal self using meditation and uniquely unfolds greater awareness.

The third shared aim is that in this conversation between conscious and unconscious self, both depth psychology and Zen Buddhism offer a path to more mature development and self-expression based on integrating self and Self. Self with a capital "S" is used in this paper to indicate the transcendent, more expansive part of human awareness or psyche that reflects, illuminates, and contains one's more personally identified personality or self. According to both disciplines, studying and allowing the whole Self to be more fully known and expressed represents the human opportunity to be free from the acting out behaviors that neither lead to more mature personal expression nor further meeting life goals.

There are several specific ways that Zen meditation enhances self-awareness and makes unconscious material more accessible and subject to transformation. First, through meditation practice one develops heightened attention. With heightened attention a larger field of awareness called the universal Self or the Abode of Radiant Light is cultivated. Once this awareness is activated, subtle patterns are noticed, and one may consciously observe the process by which one tightens the grip (of clinging or identifying) on neurotic patterns. Second, one uses this light to burn off delusive patterns. Both the quantity and the quality of awareness are used to transform neurotic patterns. Third, through relying on and returning to universal Self there is a transfer of energy from small self to larger Self. One continuously releases identification with the previous self-narrative, the personal self based on family history and defensive constructions. Instead, one learns to return to identifying with illuminated awareness, a more reliable Self.

DISCOVERING UNIVERSAL SELF: THE ABODE OF RADIANT LIGHT

In meditation practice one is taught to unify awareness by focusing on awareness itself and not the contents of awareness. Zen meditation instruction describes the mind as "sky" and the arising thoughts, feelings, and sensation as clouds in that sky. A meditator is taught to focus on the sky itself, the essence of mind rather than the contents of mind. Focusing on awareness itself, one becomes aware of illumination. In meditation, one starts with this personal light—however fleeting— to begin to study the self.

Zen master Yunmen said, "Everyone has a light."[6] Dōgen's disciple Koun Ejo (1198–1280) gave these meditation instructions to facilitate contact with the vast illuminated Self:

> Do not be pulled by a particular state of mind or by an object. Do not rely on intellect or wisdom. Do not carry in your hands what you have learned in the *sangha* hall [Buddhist instructions to the community]. Cast your body and mind into the *Great Komyozo* [treasure house of divine light] and never look back. Neither seek to be enlightened nor drive away delusions. Neither hate the arising of thoughts, nor love thoughts and identify with them. Just sit stably and calmly. Just sit as if you were a boundless empty sky or a ball of fire.[7]

In Zen meditation, study and transformation of the self occur through intimacy with what is described as the Abode of Radiant Light. One strengthens awareness for its own sake—without a specific goal—and then uses this illuminated awareness to reflect the arising thoughts.

Through careful and attentive practice and repeated intimacy with the vast and luminous quality of bare awareness, the light of the mind becomes stronger, brighter, and more penetrating, illuminating and transforming the activity of the mind. As thoughts are reflected in meditation, strengthened awareness allows them greater space within which to arise. More deeply hidden layers of mind continue to be revealed and reflected in this space. One begins to see that she or he is not angry, but anger is arising within a more spacious and illuminated mind. The "I" is not angry; the "I" is the space in which anger arises.

There are not two minds—one thinking and one that is watching. The meditative experience reveals one mind, simultaneously thinking and feeling; one develops a greater capacity to observe ongoing thinking and feeling activity. While self-reflection may occur quite naturally, Zen meditation provides an opportunity to enhance the reflective or observing quality of the mind. Depth psychology offers the therapist's mind as additional space for a patient's self-reflection. Meditation practice offers the development of careful serene attention which observes the surface of the mind and finds the radiant light that illuminates deeper hidden levels and facilitates change. The thinking, acting, and emoting mind is called the "small self." That which is capable of observing and illuminating is called the universal Self: the self which settles upon the Self.

Zen meditation refines and heightens the experience of the awareness that permeates consciousness. Light shining in the mind as formless awareness enhances the ability to self-reflect. Through meditation, heightened intimacy with awareness itself, one becomes more familiar with one's own light. Each of us may learn to access, enhance, and enjoy this light in meditation practice. One returns to the light and rests the mind within it. At first, one may only be able to observe arising thoughts and sensations. As one repeats meditation, one develops a more intimate contact with the essence of unformed awareness. One simply rests there and allows the experience of pure present awareness to grow and permeate the body and mind. Then more subtle mental formations are seen and understood as they arise; hidden bodily sensations are also revealed. Sometimes, a connection is experienced between the mental formations—thoughts and feelings—that reveal habitual patterns of defensiveness. The experience of resting in unformed awareness is pleasant and seems to allow freedom from the cluttered and hectic experience of one's everyday consciousness.

The experience of resting in awareness can be likened to a light hypnotic trance. Like the patient attention of a kind therapist, this awareness may observe thought patterns without judgment. The observing mind has its own healing effect on the practitioner's level of tension and defensiveness. Just as the trusting acceptance of a therapist gives us confidence to encounter deeper levels of conflict, resting in awareness allows a practitioner the confidence to access deeper levels of internal conflict. Increased familiarity with the technique of resting in awareness results in increased conscious access to more subtle thought patterns.

Reviewing a practical example of how concentrative energy can illuminate habitual patterns helps to clarify the process. In this particular case, a female meditator reported projecting a parental relationship on a meditation teacher. Her father's physical abuse and his early death induced severe conflict when she experienced her meditation teacher's anger. This Zen student experienced the teacher's correction as if it were her previous abuse and would lead to the loss of her teacher as had been the case with her childhood loss of her father. She repeatedly experienced her teacher's anger as unresolved and abusive emotional criticism from her long-deceased father.

By developing calm presence with her arising feelings, she was able to make the connection to her earlier loss. She noticed how she continued to suffer from fear of losing the teacher. Even after she recounted all this to her teacher, she noticed that her reactive feelings to her teacher's corrections persisted. She continued to note her feelings, to see the connections, and to make adjustments to her relationship with her teacher through observing her feelings and the arising of fear. The first stage of practicing with her trauma helped her to be less reactive to her teacher's corrections.

In this case, conscious body-mind connections facilitated intimacy and then transformed conflictual patterns. If bodily sensations are connected to thought patterns and defensive reactions, one can use this more relaxed state to experiment with not reacting or letting go of the defensive posture. While this practice of letting go may begin in the safe state of meditation, it may be carried over to more active engagement in everyday life. In the Zen environment, we call this process "taking the practice off the cushion." With growing stability and access to this enhanced awareness, this Zen student began to adjust her reactions to her teacher and to other people and situations in real time. Contact with the light acted as a gentle and wise therapist symbolically accompanying and informing daily encounters during personally sensitive and emotionally complex situations.

DEVELOPING AND USING THE ENERGY OF UNIVERSAL SELF

The second way that meditation transforms habitual neurotic patterns is through creating a more concentrated awareness. Awareness is both quantitatively and qualitatively changed in meditation. Meditation training intensifies awareness and the capacity of the mind to become a transformative power. Just as a laser beam is capable of burning off diseased tissue, amplifying concentration changes it qualitatively so that it can dissolve deluded or infantile thought patterns. The usual level of mental concentration is sufficient for processing the tasks of ordinary daily activity. With steady application of concentration practice and study, cognitive ability is increased quantitatively, and information processing becomes more efficient. In the same way that we develop intellectual capacity, practicing meditation also builds a qualitatively different kind of mental energy that can encounter, highlight, and dissolve mental suffering.

Just as a person with specialized training may develop the capacity to solve particular problems, those who meditate train their minds to develop greater and different spiritual potential through relying on the radiant light. Meditation practice exercises the mind. The strengthened mind becomes a suffering-transforming energy beam. The focused beam of attention can burn through the clouds of self-clinging to one's own narrative, delusions, and unwholesome patterns. This transformed awareness energy is developed from meditative training. When this awareness is directly focused on delusions arising in one's own mind, it can release stubborn patterns instantaneously. More than just the experience of seeing the source of the problem, this energy both penetrates and dissolves. The energy developed and heightened through meditation becomes like the strength of sunlight dissolving the frozen energy of water trapped in ice. As Zen master Koun Ejo taught, "if you trustfully open yourself to it [the treasury of light] . . . you will not need to ask someone else what is true or false. You will be as intimate with Reality as if you were to come face to face with your grandfather in a town."[8] Accordingly, one develops another way of knowing and being that is based on the light.

In our practical example, the Zen student continued observing her conflicted feelings and patterns with her teacher. Even though she had identified the pattern, and even though she had described the pattern to the teacher, she still experienced her teacher as if he were the equivalent of an earlier loss of father. Emotional distress over the teacher's angry corrections lessened but were still associated with earlier wounds. The student reported that she did not turn away from the arising suffering. She returned to meditative awareness with full knowledge of the previous trauma and the emotionally charged projection onto her teacher and his corrections.

The student later reported that during an extended meditation retreat, while fully experiencing her dilemma, the entire emotional suffering suddenly and instantaneously dissolved. She described it "like a bubble popping in a flash of light." The dysphoric mood was instantly alleviated and the relationship with the teacher found new adult footing which has continued for more than a decade. The entire conflict changed in one moment of deep meditation. There was an insight accompanying this immediate and powerful illumination and transformation. She realized that she was no longer the child who had suffered both the abuse and the loss. Previously she had consciously recognized this, but the unconscious self-constructions, frozen in time, were suddenly revealed and dissolved. A qualitative shift occurred that affected all of her relationships.

### Releasing Old Patterns: Relying on Universal Self

The healing power of awareness, refined through meditation, develops in tandem with the third transformative element of Zen meditation: identifying with awareness or universal Self, instead of identifying with one's narrative or current difficulties. Uchiyama explains,

> Usually we do not understand these circumstances of the present moment as the scenery that unfolds within the universal Self . . . When we see everything as the scenery and circumstances of the here and now . . . we function as the universal self within this moment.[9]

One tends to self-identify with a life story, a particular unfolding of events and characters that have shaped one's personal self. Through meditation one revisits that which is aware, also called the universal Self. Awareness includes knowledge of personal events, but meditative awareness extends far beyond the personal story. The Self accessed through meditation is universal unbounded awareness. It reflects, illuminates, and recalls personal events without being limited to identifying with the personal specifics. This Self is the vast environment in which the personal mind resides and personal life unfolds. In Zen meditation one releases identification with personal mind and its personal story as "self." Instead, one learns to return to becoming the environment of awareness as the true Self. This process more fully explains Uchiyama's instruction, one lives his or her life as the "universal Self."

A meditator who has experienced and reexperienced this big Self, big mind, observing self, or universal Self gains ready access to this Self in the midst of everyday activity. One can step back into this vast and spacious Self and, in so doing, loosen the painful grip of self-identification and its consequent suffering. It is as if the wounds of past injuries are washed in healing balm every time one reenters this universal Self. Habitual clinging to injury and dysfunction make way for new emotional flexibility and behaviors.

The meditator in our example above reported the persistence of emotions relating to earlier abuse and loss arising with less intensity after the initial dissolution in meditation. When the fear of loss and the projection of earlier parental abuse arose, the practitioner remembered to enter the "ocean of Buddhahood" or the Abode of the Radiant Light. She became able to return to and rely on this spacious and illuminated mind as her true identity. She would access and reflect this light on a current situation—becoming the universal Self.

There are two ways one could see this process: as a distribution of internal energy from an internal source to specific smaller channels or as allowing the external "ocean of Buddhahood" into one's own consciousness. Light energy (like water) flows into smaller tributaries which nourish the person's experience. The circulation of energy is similar to how the heart pumps the blood to the arteries and then from the arteries down into the smallest capillaries, where at the cellular level nutrients are delivered and toxins removed. The experience of the radiant light is distributed and reexperienced in the most immediate personal everyday life interactions.

From the perspective of entering the ocean of Buddhahood, one sees that the ocean gradually permeates and softens experiences in the deepest places. This ocean reaches places that are like stains, knots where personal experiences have become hardened. One allows the ebb and flow of this ocean to soften these knots or wash out these stains. Meditative transformation should not result in repression or a fugue state into some enlightened persona. Rather, the quantitative, qualitative, and sudden transformations from self- to Self-awareness need gradual integration into personal habits. The island remains connected to the earth at the bottom of the ocean, but there is a constant communication between the ocean and the island, and the shore where they meet is transformed. Depth psychology effects healing through a gradual, personal, and trusting relationship with a therapist while Zen meditation is a progressive entry into, and personal intimacy with, the ocean of Buddhahood, the universal Self.

## NOTES

1. C. G. Jung, "The Psychology of the Transference," in *The Collected Works of C. G. Jung,* vol. 16, *The Practice of Psychotherapy* (Princeton, NJ: Princeton University Press, 1966), § 366.

2. Koun Ejo, "Komyozo Zammai," in *Shikantaza,* trans. Shohaku Okumura (Kyoto: Kyoto Zen Center, 1987), p. 79.

3. Eihei Dōgen and Kosho Uchiyama, *From the Zen Kitchen to Enlightenment,* trans. Tom Wright (New York: Weatherhill, 1983), p. 87.

4. C. G. Jung, "Symbols and the Interpretation of Dreams," in *The Collected Works of C. G. Jung,* vol. 18, *The Symbolic Life* (Princeton, NJ: Princeton University Press, 1976), § 512.

5. Shohaku Okumura, *Realizing Genjokoan* (Somerville, MA: Wisdom Publications, 2010), p. 2.

6. Yuanwu, Thomas Cleary, and Jonathan Christopher Cleary, *The Blue Cliff Record* (Boston: Shambhala, 2005), p. 472.

7. Ejo, "Komyozo Zammai," p. 78.

8. Yuanwu, Cleary, and Cleary, *The Blue Cliff Record,* p. 79.

9. Kosho Uchiyama, *Opening the Hand of Thought,* trans. Tom Wright (Somerville, MA: Wisdom Publications, 2004), p. 133.

# CALMING THE MIND (*AN-HSIN*)
## THE EARLY CHINESE ZEN BUDDHISM AND PSYCHOTHERAPY

SHOJI MURAMOTO

### BUDDHISM TRANSMITTED EASTWARD AND ITS CULTURAL ADAPTATION

A distinctive feature of Western, especially American, Buddhism is the strong interest in its interface with psychotherapy. Those who practice both Buddhism and psychotherapy are common in America, but rarely found in China or Japan. More than eighty years ago, in a psychological commentary for a book on Chinese alchemy, Carl Gustav Jung warned Westerners attracted to Eastern religions against losing themselves in a mist of ideas inconceivable to the Western mind.[1] His concern now appears to have been unwarranted because Westerners do not seem to have been lost through the study and the practice of Eastern spirituality but, on the contrary, to have found an identity. They seem to have demonstrated the truth of a traditional

Shoji Muramoto, Ph.D., is an editorial committee member of the *Journal of Humanistic Psychology* and was a professor at Hanazono University and Kobe City Universities of Foreign Studies. He is the coeditor of *Awakening and Insight: Buddhism and Psychotherapy* (2001), based on the 1999 international conference in Kyoto organized with P. Young-Eisendrath, which includes his translation from the German original of the 1957 Jung-Hisamatsu conversation. He is the author of *Jung and Goethe* (1992), *Jung and Faust* (1993), and *The Encounter of the West with Buddhism* (1998).

saying, "Buddhism is transmitted eastward," because, born in India, it was transmitted to China and Japan, and finally across the Pacific Ocean to America.

Buddhism has characteristically developed by adapting itself to the culture of a country to which it has been transmitted and creating a new style there. There is a general, though not necessarily correct, impression that Buddhism was speculative in India, practical in China, aesthetic in Japan, and is now psychological in America. The increase in the number of books published in English on the relationship between Buddhism and psychotherapy during these decades is itself remarkable.[2]

The enthusiasm of Western psychotherapists for Buddhist practices mostly stems from practical and existential concerns: they expect from Buddhism a new perspective on human life that may make their clinical practice more effective and provide a spirituality more appealing to Western values. As is often the case in a situation where a practical and existential concern is dominant, however, psychologists may neglect or at least be indifferent to the history and diversity of Buddhism, especially Zen.[3] Americans may imagine Buddhism to be an ahistorical system of theory and practice.

Japanese intellectuals affiliated with the philosophy of the Kyoto School, especially Daisetzu Teitaro Suzuki (鈴木大拙, 1870–1966)—if Hu-shi (胡適, 1891–1962), his Chinese opponent, is right—deprived Zen Buddhism of its historicity. Suzuki provided the West with a version of Buddhism that could be an alternative spirituality demanding neither intellectual renunciation nor blind faith. As a result, psychotherapists as represented by Jung and Erich Fromm became interested in Zen, and the subsequent generations have followed suit.[4]

Questions may arise: Is the concept of mind not different between Buddhism and Western psychotherapy? Are Buddhist and Western psychologies really compatible? We may also ask whether Jung's concern has already lost any validity as Buddhism has been popularized in the West.

CALMING THE MIND (*AN-HSIN*) AS THE CORE OF ZEN BUDDHISM

There is a famous legendary dialogue between Bodhidharma (菩提達摩, d. 532), the alleged founder of Zen Buddhism, and Hui'-k'o (慧可, 487–593), his disciple who was to become the second patriarch of Chinese Zen Buddhism.[5] One day Hui'-k'o asked his teacher seated in meditation how he could calm his restless mind. The master replied, "Bring me your mind and I will calm it." Hui'-k'o said, "Try as I may, I cannot find it." At this Bodhidharma spoke again, "Your mind is calmed."

Heinrich Dumolin (1905–1995), a Jesuit theologian well versed in Zen Buddhism, regards this dialogue as prefiguring the essence and formation of the Zen school.[6] In fact, more than one thousand years later, Bankei Yotaku (盤珪永啄,1622–1693), a Japanese Rinzai Zen Master, treated a samurai suffering from impatience in the same way as Bodhidharma had treated Hui'-k'o. He made the samurai aware of the unborn mind, which is nothing but the Buddha mind.

Seizan Yanagida (柳田聖山, 1922–2006), a leading expert on the history of Zen Buddhism, sees in the dialogue between Bodhidharma and Hui'-k'o the prototype of subsequent *mondos*.[7] A *mondo* (問答), literally meaning questions and answers, is a typical energetic dialogue, which later provided Zen masters during the Sung Dynasty (960–1279) with koans. What Hui'-k'o asked for and Bodhidharma claimed to have given him is a calm mind—for which the original Chinese word is *an-hsin* (安心), transliterated into Japanese as *an-jin*. The dialogue between Bodhidharma and Hui'-k'o has been traditionally called *anjin-mondo* (安心問答) in Japan. This Buddhist term *an-jin* was later secularized to be read as *anshin,* a word Japanese people today use to describe "relief," related to such terms in clinical and developmental psychology as *security* (Harry Stack Sullivan) and *attachment* (John Bowlby). *An-jin* is, however, more fundamental and metaphysical than *anshin*. In Zen Buddhism, Chinese or Japanese, *an-hsin* or *an-jin* is virtually identical with enlightenment.

To unpack the meaning of *an-hsin*, we must become familiar with the Mahāyāna Buddhist concept of mind expressed in the Chinese word, *hsin* (心) transliterated as *shin* and translated into Japanese as *kokoro*.

### THE TRANSMISSION OF BUDDHISM TO CHINA AND ITS ADAPTATION TO CHINESE SPIRITUALITY

Buddhism was transmitted from India via the Western Regions to China several centuries before Bodhidharma's arrival there. Chinese are generally known to avoid the supernatural and the demonic, but people in northern China venerated foreign Buddhist monks who displayed miracles as signs of attainment to a high level of Samadhi. At the same time, the political authority of Confucianism was weakened and Taoism developed in China. In early Buddhism the cultivation of miraculous powers was taken to be the practice of compassion, and so it is no wonder that Buddhism developed in China under the strong influence of Taoism.

From the late second to the fifth century both Mahāyāna and Theravāda texts were translated into Chinese by foreign monks from the Western Regions. What attracted Chinese intellectuals, however, was the wisdom teachings of various *prajnaparamita* sutras in Mahāyāna Buddhism. The foreign translators as well as Chinese intellectuals, especially those involved in the third-century spiritual movement called the Study of Mystery (*hsüan-hsüeh* 玄学), adapted Buddhism to traditional Chinese spirituality, especially the wisdom teaching of Lao-tzu (老子) and Chuang-tzu (荘子). Foreign translators and their disciples in China all reinterpreted emptiness (*sunyata,* 空)— the true nature of all beings in the Buddhist view—as fundamental nothingness (*pen-wu,* 本無). This Taoist concept has nothing to do with modern nihilism but rather the metaphysical substance full of energy, the basis of the subject or self in the Chinese sense. Thusness (*tathata*) and enlightenment (*bodhi*) were likewise equated with non-action (*wu-wei,* 無為), a key concept in Lao-tzu's philosophy.

*Ko-I* (格義), this syncretistic method of the Chinese interpretation of Buddhism, was later sharply criticized by Seng-chao (僧肇, 384–414). Unsatisfied with Taoism, he assisted Kumarajiva (344–413) in the translation of Mahāyāna, especially *prajnaparamita* sutras, and became "the first Chinese to capture the quintessence of the Madhyamika philosophy in a truly Chinese way."[8] Quoting Indian philosopher and enlightened teacher Nāgārjuna (ca. 150–250), he clearly distinguished fundamental nothingness in Taoism from *sunyata* in Mahāyāna Buddhism, in which all things are related to each other through dependent origination without any metaphysical substance, positive or negative.

Yet Yanagida points out that Seng-chao, a practice-oriented Chinese author, was not entirely free from the syncretistic interpretation of Buddhism. Seng-chao writes, "How can Tao be found in some far place? All things are real." He was primarily concerned with the "true subject" as the embodiment of perfect wisdom. In Yanagida's view, Seng-chao interpreted the Vimalakirti Sutra not in an Indian but in a Chinese way, for he read "demonstrating nirvana without giving up kleshas" in a way that retains and stresses the bond with this world.[9]

Thus Seng-chao proposed the doctrine of substance (*t'i*, 体) and function (*yung*, 用) in which all phenomena are understood to be the function of *t'i*. Substance and function are conceptually distinguished but virtually inseparable from each other. Despite his criticism of syncretism Seng-chao himself actually provided the philosophical basis for the subsequent development of a uniquely Chinese Buddhism. In *Treatise of the Awakening of Faith in Mahāyāna* (*Ta-cheng ch'i-hsin lun*, 大乗起信論), translated by Paramartha in the sixth century, form (*xiang*, 相) is added to substance and function as the third element, inseparable from them.

While Seng-chao regarded the path to enlightenment as a gradual progress, Tao-Sheng (道生, ca. 360–434), another of Kumarajiva's followers, has been called the actual founder of the Zen school because of his doctrine of sudden enlightenment. Tao-Sheng prompted a split between the Northern School and the Southern School in the late seventh century. This split was represented by Shen-hsiu (神秀, 605–706) and Ho-tse Shen-hui (荷沢神会, 670–762), the editor of *The Platform Sutra of the Sixth Patriarch*. These schools disagreed not so much about the methodology of meditation but about the view of the mind.[10]

What provided Tao-Sheng with the platform for claiming sudden insight was his encounter with the *Mahayananirvana* sutra which says there is a universal Buddha Nature (*Buddhata*) in all sentient beings. This idea contrasts with *sunyata* as established in Madhyamika. Buddha Nature resonates more closely with the Atman of Upanishad philosophy. Suddenness of enlightenment here does not so much refer to a short time spent in reaching enlightenment, but to the full realization of one's Buddha Nature.

In the Zen tradition, Buddha Nature is generally synonymous with Buddha Mind. There has been, however, no evidence which suggests the direct link between Tao-Sheng's notion and the Zen school.[11] Claims for Buddha Nature and for sudden awakening are said to arise from direct experience, without words, transmitted from master to disciple along the Zen lineage going back to the Buddha.

It has been traditionally believed to be Bodhidharma (d. 532) who brought to China "the seal of the Buddha's mind" symbolized by the robe and the begging bowl. Known as the twenty-eighth Indian patriarch and the first Chinese patriarch of Zen Buddhism, Bodhidharma stands historically at the decisive turning point from Indian to Chinese Buddhism. Despite the opaqueness of his historical identity, or rather because of the legendary or even mythical character of the dharma lineage, Bodhidharma has in the Zen tradition acquired a position almost equal to the Buddha.[12]

And yet, no genuine writings by Bodhidharma have been uncovered, even among those discovered in Tunhuang in the beginning of the twentieth century. But among those from Tunhuang, *The Treatise on Two Entrances and Four Acts* provides the oldest and the most important information about Bodhidharma and his first followers, as well as records of sayings alleged to be his and theirs. This text might have originated in the seventh century when Tao-hsin (道信, 580–651), the fourth patriarch, and Hung-jen (弘忍, 610–674), the fifth patriarch, began to be officially recognized as having established the Zen school. Around this time, Bodhidharma began to function as the founding figure who has continued to be elaborated, in various legendary ways, depending on the historical development of Zen Buddhism.

*Entrance* in the title of the text mentioned above refers to enlightenment. Its editor, Tan-lin (曇林, 506–574), points out in the preface that one entrance to the way or the calming of the mind (*an-hsin*) is principle(*li*, 理), the other being practice (*xing*, 行) as the working through of principle in everyday life. Entrance as enlightenment, expressed thus, means the Buddha is none other than one's mind, a conviction expressed by almost all subsequent Zen masters. The mind here does not merely have the potential of becoming a Buddha; it is already a Buddha. The discipline of Zen, accordingly, mainly consists in not so much helping the student become a Buddha, but in making him realize the primordial fact that he is already a Buddha. Strictly speaking, to be unconscious in Mahāyāna Buddhism is to be ignorant or unaware of this condition. Suzuki claims, therefore, that the Chinese character 心 denoting mind (*hsin*) is both the hallmark and the principle of the Zen school beginning with Bodhidharma.[13]

While the Indian form of mindfulness meditation (*satipatthäna*) was still practiced in early Chinese Buddhism, wall-gazing (*pi-kuan*, 壁観), a new meditation brought by Bodhidharma to China, was nothing but entrance as *an-hsin*. The "wall" here is actually a metaphor for the mind into which no dust or illusion can enter according to the practice of *prajnaparamita* teaching.

Strictly speaking, as Yanagida suggests, this approach might radically reject all disciplines, including *zazen*, as unnecessary tricks initiated by the disturbed mind.[14] However, from the viewpoint of the Lotus sutra, another important text of Zen Buddhism, practices are not to be simply rejected but rather to be properly evaluated and used as *upayas* or skillful means for enlightenment. This conflict about practices can also be applied to psychotherapy techniques.

### BUDDHISM AND WESTERN PSYCHOLOGY

We realize now that the affinity of Buddhism, especially Zen, with psychology is no Western phenomenon but belongs to the nature of Buddhism. Chinese Zen Buddhism is both practical and metaphysical. While Western psychotherapy traditions theoretically postulate some metaphysical substance that is inaccessible empirically, such as libido or psychic energy, the substance in Chinese Buddhist metaphysics can and must be experienced and demonstrated in function and form. The Western split between religion and science does not fit comfortably with the tradition of Chinese Zen. We must be careful not to make naïve connections between Western psychology and Zen because the former seems to have nothing corresponding to the kind of mind which Bodhidharma asked Hui'-k'o to bring him. Western psychology and psychotherapy are concerned with mental and psychological phenomena and not the mind itself. Although Buddhism rejects faith in a personal deity, it demands the awakening of faith in the mind. Otherwise the doctrine of sudden enlightenment would be meaningless and misleading. The mind in Buddhism has, therefore, both empirical and transcendental or at least spiritual aspects that are hardly to be found in Western psychotherapies.

Jungian psychology with its concept of Self may indeed be the most promising partner in the dialogue between Western psychology and Buddhism. Buddhists, however, are interested in neither the distinction nor the relation between the ego and the self, as Jungians are. Additionally, some Jungians who separate in the Kantian way archetypal images from the archetype in itself (*an sich*) might find the Mahāyāna ontology in its Chinese version of substance, function, and form to be alien. Others, sympathetic with Gnosticism, might not agree with the Mahāyāna concept of mind as essentially pure in itself and so nothing but a Buddha.

Further, psychotherapists frequently find Zen discourses too abstract sounding and insensitive for people living in today's apocalyptic age.[15] Zen phrases such as "being a master wherever you are" from Lin-chi (臨済, d. 866), even when accompanied by years of meditation, may not induce freedom from repetition compulsions or unconscious expressions of traumatic or other disturbances from early life. Yet, Buddhists could present a counter-argument that psychotherapy only makes the patient keep on wandering in the forest of samsara without finding a way out.

A touchstone for the encounter of psychology with Zen Buddhism may be the conversation in 1958 between Jung and Shin'ichi Hisamatsu (久松真—, 1889–1980). A Japanese Zen philosopher, Hisamatsu embarrassed Jung by questioning him as to whether psychotherapy could liberate the patient from suffering in one fell swoop.[16] This sometimes frustrating conversation shows not only how hard, but also how necessary, it has been to try to reconcile Western psychology and Zen Buddhism in terms of the concept of mind and its underlying metaphysics. To see these differences from another angle may be to reactivate the tensions in early Chinese Zen Buddhism, such as the controversy between the Northern School and Southern School, on the nature of enlightenment in the modern West.

### NOTES

1. C. G. Jung, "Commentary on 'The Secret of the Golden Flower,'" in *The Collected Works of C. G. Jung*, vol. 13, *Alchemical Studies* (London: Routledge and Kegan Paul, 1967), § 3.

2. For example, Anthony Molino, *The Couch and the Tree: Dialogues in Psychoanalysis and Buddhism* (New York: North Point Press, 1998); Polly Young-Eisendrath and Shoji Muramoto, eds., *Awakening and Insight: Zen Buddhism and Psychotherapy* (East Sussex: Brunner-

Routledge, 2002); Dale Mathers, Melvin Miller, and Osamu Ando, eds., *Self and No-Self: Continuing the Dialogue between Buddhism and Psychotherapy* (London: Routledge, 2009).

3. Shoji Muramoto, "The Buddhist Concept of Mind and Body in Diversity," in Raya Jones, ed., *Body, Mind Healing after Jung* (London: Routledge, 2010), pp. 127–144.

4. C. G. Jung, "Forward to Suzuki's Introduction to Zen Buddhism," in *The Collected Works of C. G. Jung*, vol. 11, *Psychology and Religion: West and East* (London: Routledge and Kegan Paul, 1958); Daisetsu T. Suzuki, Erich Fromm, and Robert de Martino, *Zen Buddhism and Psychoanalysis* (New York: G. Allen and Unwin, 1960).

5. In *The Treatise of Two Entrances and Four Acts*, a text mentioned later in which the oldest version of the following conversation appears, it is not Bodhidharma but Hui'-k'o who claims to have calmed his disciple's mind.

6. Heinrich Dumolin, *Zen Buddhism: A History, Volume 1: India and China* (New York: Macmillan Library Reference USA, 1994), p. 92.

7. Seizan Yanagida, *Daruma* (Tokyo: Kodansha, 1981, repr. 1998), p. 141.

8. Dumolin, *Zen Buddhism*, p. 71.

9. Seizan Yanagida, *Mu no tankyu: Chugoku-Zen [The Quest for Nothingness: Chinese Zen]* (Tokyo: Kadokawa-bunko, 1969, repr. 1997), p. 106.

10. In *The Platform Sutra*, Hung-jen (601–674), the fifth patriarch, challenges his disciples to create a poem expressing the nature of the mind. In the poem by Shen-hsiu, the most highly esteemed of Hung-jen's disciples, the mind like a mirror must be always carefully wiped so that no dust is on the surface. In the counter-poem, Hui-neng (638–713), the hero of the sutra who was to become the sixth patriarch, argues that the mind as the mirror, being originally pure, cannot be tainted by dust.

11. Dumolin, *Zen Buddhism*, p. 77.

12. In the earliest reference to Bodhidharma in a text from the sixth century he appears as a pious monk from Persia simply praising many beautiful temples in Lo-yang. But in *Further Biographies of Eminent Monks* from the seventh century he is presented as a prince of a Brahman family in southern India.

13. Daistsu Teitaro Suzuki, "Daruma-zen to sono shisoteki haikei [The Intellectual Background of Dharma Zen]," in *Suzuki Daisetsu Zenshu [Complete Works of Daisetsu Suzuki]*, vol. 2 (Tokyo: Iwnami-shoten, 1951, 2000), pp. 57, 59, 63.

14. "Shoki-zenshu to shikan-shisou [Early Zen Buddhism and samatha-vipasyna]," in *Yanagida Seizan Shu dai 2-kan [Collection of Seizan Yanagida's Works]*, vol. 2 (1975; repr. Kyoto: Hozonkan, 1999), pp. 66–67.

15. In the ongoing catastrophe precipitated by the accident at nuclear reactors in Fukushima on March 11, 2011, Eihei-ji, a Zen temple founded by Dōgen (1200–1253) that is the center of Japanese Soto school, criticized itself for its cooperation with Kansai Electric Company as being contrary to the Buddhist spirit of compassion. At the company's request, the temple had proposed the names of two great Bodhisattvas, Monjusri (Jap. Monju) and Samantabhadra (Jap. Fugen), for two fast breeder reactors the company had been constructing in the same prefecture. In November 2011, the temple organized a symposium to prevent subsequent generations from inheriting our follies.

16. "The Jung-Hisamatsu Conversation: A Translation from Aniela Jaffé's Original German Protocol," trans. Shoji Muramoto in cooperation with Polly Young-Eisendrath and Jan Middeldorf, in Anthony Molino, *The Couch and the Tree*, p. 44.

# IDEALIZING, SUGGESTION, AND PROJECTION

# SUGGESTION AND TRUTH IN PSYCHOANALYSIS AND BUDDHISM

ROBERT CAPER

## SUGGESTION AND SYMPTOMS

Psychoanalysis was born from suggestion, itself an expression of the ancient wish, present in everyone, to control the mind—one's own and others. The *Oxford English Dictionary* defines *suggestion* as "the insinuation of a belief or impulse into the mind of a subject by words, gestures, or the like; the impulse or idea thus suggested." Unlike ordinary persuasion, the action and effects of suggestion are mainly unconscious. Suggestion is far more pervasive and subtle than one would suppose from the old stereotype of a hypnotist instructing a subject to do or feel something. It may be conveyed even without words—for example, by demeanor, facial expression, or tone of voice. Since it occurs outside awareness, it acts without regard to the conscious intentions of both parties; one need not intend to practice suggestion in order to do so. For reasons that will become clear as

Robert Caper, M.D., is a psychoanalyst and assistant clinical professor of psychiatry at UCLA School of Medicine. He is the author of *Immaterial Facts: Freud's Discovery of Psychic Reality and Klein's Development of His Work* (1988), *A Mind of One's Own* (1999), and *Building Out into the Dark* (2010). He is the author of numerous papers on psychoanalysis and has lectured extensively in North America, Europe, Australia, and Latin America. He currently practices in Vermont.

we go along, the forces of suggestion operate especially powerfully in the parent-child relationship, the doctor-patient relationship, and the teacher-student relationship. Because of this, psychoanalysis has been struggling ever since its beginnings to rise above suggestion, with its seductive promise of *taming* the unruly mind, and instead to pursue the goal of *exploring* the mind.

Freud began his clinical career in the 1880s as a psychiatrist practicing suggestion. In those days, medical suggestion consisted of little more than using the brute force of the suggestionist's personality to push an idea into the patient's mind. From the beginning, Freud was uncomfortable with this practice, as he indicated years later when he recalled witnessing the technique of his mentor Hippolyte Bernheim:

> I remember even then feeling a muffled hostility to this tyranny of suggestion. When a patient who showed himself unamenable was met with the shout: "what are you doing? Vous vous contre-suggestionnez!" I said to myself this was an evident injustice and an act of violence. For the man certainly had a right to counter-suggestions if people were trying to subdue him with suggestions.[1]

Freud found a potential solution to this dilemma when he heard from his older colleague Josef Breuer about a young female patient beset with dramatic hysterical symptoms, whom Breuer would visit daily for sessions of what the patient, Anna O., called "chimney sweeping." Anna would recount for Breuer the events of the day, with special emphasis on those that had upset her. Breuer would listen patiently, following which Anna would experience a definite, although temporary, relief of her symptoms. They would repeat the procedure the following day, with similar results. Interruptions of the treatment would lead to deterioration of Anna's condition, and its resumption to improvement.

Freud was impressed enough by Breuer's experience with Anna to persuade him to collaborate on a book, *Studies on Hysteria*, which chronicled Breuer's treatment of her, along with Freud's treatment of a number of cases of hysteria using Breuer's method.[2] Freud was a theoretician who was intensely interested in how this method worked primarily for the light that would thus be shed on the operation of the unconscious mind. Unlike Breuer, he was not interested in symptomatic relief; he was after a radical cure. He concluded *Studies on Hysteria* with a theoretical exposition about the causes and treatment of hysteria—his so-called seduction theory of hysteria.

Breuer seems to have been a passive and sympathetic listener for Anna. His method of treatment was far less aggressive and intrusive than Bernheim's method of suggestion. Freud, however, was interested in testing his theories of hysteria. Accordingly, he began to delve actively into the events surrounding his patients' symptomatic episodes and to exert what he called "pressure" on them to overcome their supposed repressions and to recall the historical sexual trauma that had, as he thought, produced their illness. Freud's technique was apparently quite forceful (at one point he actually exerted physical pressure on the patient's forehead to induce her to remember), and it is clear at least in retrospect that it constituted a form of suggestion no less vigorous and intrusive than Bernheim's.

Freud eventually abandoned his pressure technique, but not until he had at his disposal a tool that allowed him to practice suggestion in a way that was both more subtle and more powerful than direct suggestion: transference. Soon after its discovery, he realized that instead of pressuring his patients to recall what he wished them to recall, he could exploit what he called the "positive transference" to similar effect.

## Positive Transference

The positive transference is a repetition of the patient's childhood relationship to a trusted and loved parent. Freud found he could rely on the patient's love for the analyst-parent to motivate the patient to acknowledge the repressed sexual impulses and traumas that he supposed the patient had. Freud's famous dictum that analysis was a "cure through love" referred not to the analyst's love for the patient, but to the patient's love for the analyst.[3] The patient would remember what the analyst wanted him to *because* the analyst wanted him to and because the patient loved the analyst in a childlike way and wanted to please the analyst the way a child wants to please its parents.

The patient's susceptibility to suggestion depended on this love and also on the fact that when he relaxed into the role of a child in the analysis, he also regressed into a childlike state of mind, which included a childlike belief in the analyst's superior knowledge and wisdom. The patient was actively looking to the analyst to cure him and would respond strongly to even the subtlest of hints from the analyst that he was being a "good patient," moving in the right direction (or, conversely, a "bad" one moving in the wrong direction).

The positive transference converts the analyst from a reasonable person, with whom one can have a discussion on more or less equal terms, adult to adult, into an idealized figure and a brandisher of parental rewards.

The discovery of transference as the basis of suggestion allowed Freud to step back from suggestion and, having distanced himself, to see it from a new and fruitful perspective. It was now possible for him to engage the patient in a way that was quite distinct from the ancient tradition of suggestion. However, while Freud opened this doorway, he did not fully step through it. He appears to have analyzed the transference selectively, interpreting only those aspects of it that interfere with the patient's "cooperation" in the analysis but leaving untouched those that promoted it.

This seems to have been about as far as Freud could go. Despite his penetrating and powerful discoveries regarding the psychological basis of suggestion, he was unable to abandon it in practice. Suggestion continued to bewitch him, and the possibility of doing psychoanalysis without exploiting its power remained unrealized.

### BEYOND SUGGESTION

It was left to others to break the spell, and they did so with two developments. The first was the discovery of realistic projective identification by the British psychoanalysts Melanie Klein, Wilfred Bion, and Paula Heimann.[4] *Realistic projective identification* is a term used to name the phenomenon in which one person is able to induce a specific mental state in another person. Cheering someone up or making them feel jealous, or envious, or depressed, or excited are all examples of the operation of realistic projective identification. It usually operates outside the awareness of either party. The term is cumbersome for historical reasons, and no one has come up with an acceptable replacement, but the idea itself is simple enough.

The discovery of realistic projective identification led to a radical revision of the original psychoanalytic assumption of a mind existing independent of other minds. Our states of mind do not arise only from within but from the impact of other minds as well. Of course, the phenomena of suggestion and suggestibility already implied this, but it took some time for psychoanalysts to appreciate the full extent of these implications. One of them is that people in close emotional contact frequently induce moods, feelings, and other mental states, wittingly or unwittingly, in one another. A mind in contact with another is not operating on its own, and a mind not in contact with another is not a mind. Suggestion, if we take it in the broad sense of something not deliberate or consciously intended, is universal in human affairs. And in psychoanalysis, as in any other relationship, it is practiced by both parties.

Realistic projective identification provides a basis for the psychoanalyst to understand a patient not simply by deciphering hidden meanings in words and gestures, like code breakers, but by close examination of the analyst's experiences as they arise when the analyst is in contact with the patient. The impact of this discovery is hard to overestimate. It transformed psychoanalysis from an exercise in puzzle solving—discovering which concept fits which patient—into a free exploration of the mind through an examination of living experience.

### The Need for Truth

The second development that has helped move psychoanalysis away from suggestion is the idea, introduced by Klein and explored most extensively by Bion and James Grotstein, that the mind needs the truth the way the body needs food.[5] This notion is a major extension of Freud's reality principle, which holds that contact with reality—that is, experiencing things as they are—is essential to the survival of the organism. This seems indisputably true when one considers, for example, that lack of awareness of the reality of hunger or of the concrete reality of food sources would rapidly lead to starvation and physical death.

Bion extended this idea to include the mind's need for contact via something like intuition with an intangible reality, variously called noumena, things-in-themselves, ultimate reality, truth, the infinite, and the godhead. Without such contact, he argued, the mind would wither and die just as the body would without food. None of these traditional terms are adequate to get at what Bion was trying to get at, and he eventually settled for calling it "O." He remarked that "it is perhaps too mathematical to call it infinity, too mystical to call it the infinite, too religious to call it the Godhead."[6] "O" cannot be known; it must rather be experienced.

If one accepts Bion's hypothesis, it becomes possible in clinical practice to rely on the patient's and analyst's need for truth to motivate them to do the work of analysis. The importance of this cannot be overstated. The abandonment of suggestion and the reliance on the patient's and analyst's need for truth frees them to conduct an exploration of the patient's mind unfettered by the need maintain a positive transference with its attendant idealization of the analyst.

Appreciation of the role of realistic projective identification in the analytic session allows the analyst to become a phenomenologist, tracking the real-time operation of what the American-born Kleinian psychoanalyst Donald Meltzer calls "the phenomenology of the consulting room," which includes the interplay of mutual suggestion in the analysis.[7]

Articulating the suggestive forces that are operating at a given moment in a psychoanalytic session undermines their power even as it illuminates them, providing that such articulation is made in the context of a psychoanalytic exploration. One of the distinguishing features of a psychoanalytic exploration, as distinct from other types of exploration, is that the psychoanalyst can help the patient understand the significance of what the psychoanalyst has articulated by virtue of the psychoanalyst's experience with the dynamics of *mis*understanding.

Even when the patient has properly understood the significance of what the analyst has articulated about suggestion, it does not disappear from the psychoanalytic relationship. Articulating the forces of suggestion merely makes them conscious. This allows both patient and analyst to become more aware of how their thoughts and emotions originate. In this way, both parties become more clear about who is who and who is doing what. To the degree that the participants in the psychoanalytic experience have succeeded in seeing the suggestive forces at work between them, they will be able to see both themselves and the other more clearly as the individuals they are. This brings them closer to the expansion of consciousness and individuation that is often considered to be a goal of clinical psychoanalysis.

Relying on a patient's desire to know the truth allows the analyst to engage the patient in a joint exploration of the truth as it arises in their experience. Therapeutic and hygienic goals, insofar as they are subtle expressions of morality (what is "healthier" or what "should be"), tend to fall away and be replaced by realistic considerations of practical consequences. Interpretations become observations designed simply to help the patient to become more conscious of the reality of who he is, without moral or therapeutic admonitions.

## CULTIVATING MINDFULNESS IN MEDITATION

These developments in psychoanalysis connect it with Buddhist practices to cultivate in the mind of the practitioner the capacity to observe experience in a purely phenomenological way. Both encourage inquiry into experience that is free of preexisting categories and explanations that might foreclose a fresh insight. A more important connection is that both disciplines are expressions of the attempt to bring experience in line with reality in its deepest sense.

There is also a direct relationship between Buddhist and psychoanalytic views of suffering. Ordinary human suffering is the consequence of being in contact with the realities of life, some of which are unavoidably painful. "Suffering" in this sense retains some of its old meaning of "tolerance." Mindfulness practice encourages this type of tolerance. The inability to accept inevitable suffering causes what might be called suffering about suffering. This secondary suffering (what Freud called "neurotic misery") is not unavoidable and in fact can be avoided by cultivating the kind of tolerance of suffering that mindfulness practice encourages and that psychoanalysis tends to bring about.

Finally, to return to the history of psychoanalysis: one of the lessons it teaches us is that unless we understand and defuse the positive transference, there is a danger that what is supposed to be a relationship dedicated to the search for truth will become one dominated by idealization and suggestion. This applies not only to the doctor-patient relationship, as in psychoanalysis, but to the teacher-student relationship, as in Buddhist training. Teachers are highly susceptible to being idealized by their students (the positive transference), and students who idealize their teachers are highly susceptible to the power of suggestion exercised wittingly or unwittingly by their teachers. If the teacher idealizes him- or herself as well, a difficult problem becomes even more difficult. The power of suggestion subverts the search for truth and magnifies the potential for many forms of abuse in the intimate relationship between teacher and student.

## NOTES

1. Sigmund Freud, "Group Psychology and the Analysis of the Ego," in *The Standard Edition of the Complete Psychological Works of Sigmund Freud*, vol. 18 (London: The Hogarth Press, 1955), p. 89.

2. Josef Breuer and Sigmund Freud, *Studies on Hysteria*, vol. 2, *The Standard Edition of the Complete Psychological Works of Sigmund Freud* (London: The Hogarth Press, 1955).

3. Peter Gay, *Freud: A Life for Our Times* (New York: W. W. Norton, 1988), p. 301.

4. Melanie Klein, "Notes on Some Schizoid Mechanisms," in *The Writings of Melanie Klein*, vol. 3, *Envy and Gratitude and Other Works 1946–1963* (London: The Hogarth Press and the Institute of Psycho-Analysis, 1975); Wilfred R. Bion, "Attacks on Linking," in *Second Thoughts: Selected Papers on Psycho-Analysis* (New York: Jason Aronson, 1967); and Paula Heimann, "On Counter-Transference," in *About Children and Children-No-Longer: Collected Papers 1942–80*, ed. Margret Tonnesmann (London: Routledge and the New Library of Psychoanalysis, 1990).

5. Melanie Klein, "The Importance of Symbol Formation in the Development of the Ego," in *The Writings of Melanie Klein*, vol. 2, *Love, Guilt and Reparation and Other Works 1921–1945* (London: The Hogarth Press and the Institute of Psycho-Analysis, 1975); Wilfred Bion, *Transformations: Change from Learning to Growth* (London: Heinemann, 1965); and James Grotstein, "The Seventh Servant: The Implications of a Truth Drive in Bion's Theory of 'O,'" *International Journal of Psychoanalysis* 85, part 5 (October 2004): 1081–1101.

6. Wilfred Bion, "Transformations," in *Seven Servants: Four Works by Wilfred R. Bion* (New York: Jason Aronson, 1977), p. 150.

7. Donald Meltzer, *Sexual States of Mind* (Perthshire: Clunie Press, 1973), p. 108.

# KNOWING OUR TEACHERS
## INTERSUBJECTIVITY AND THE BUDDHIST
## TEACHER/STUDENT DYAD

PILAR JENNINGS

L ast winter on a chilly night just after the new year, I found
myself sitting in a darkened theater at the Rubin Museum
in New York City watching *Crazy Wisdom* (2011), a
documentary about the life of Chögyam Trungpa Rinpoche. Like
most American Buddhists, I had heard the colorful stories about
his legendary theatrical pedagogy—"crazy wisdom"—and more than
a few stories about his worrisome relationship to alcohol and women.
I was curious to learn more about this teacher who had influenced
so many Western Buddhists, some of whom had gone on to become
important teachers in their own right.

Pilar Jennings is a psychoanalyst with a private practice in New York City. She received
her Ph.D. in psychiatry and religion from Union Theological Seminary and has been
working with patients and their families through the Harlem Family Institute since 2004.
Jennings is a lecturer at Columbia University and Union Theological Seminary, focusing
on the clinical applications of Buddhist meditation. Her publications include "East of
Ego: The Intersection of Narcissism and Buddhist Meditation Practice" in *Journal of
Religion and Health*, and "I've Been Waiting for You: Reflections on Analytic Pain" in
*Psychoanalytic Review*. Her most recent book is *Mixing Minds: The Power of Relationship in
Psychoanalysis and Buddhism* (2010).

As the film progressed, I felt an increasing sense of dis-ease, or *dukkha*, as it's called in Buddhist teachings. Images of a young Tibetan man trying to find his way in a foreign country filled the screen as Trungpa Rinpoche described feelings of loneliness and isolation and painful recovery from a severe car accident, possibly related to his increasingly problematic alcoholism. These scenes were quickly overshadowed by the endless testimonial of students who spoke with awe of his compelling presence and teaching methods, his depth of insight and clear enlightenment. Indeed, there were some extraordinary images: Trungpa simulating Buddhist doctrine through live enactment of military preparation for war and a vibrant otherworldly rainbow radiating above his gravesite in the days after his death.

Yet it seemed that Trungpa's students (at least those who made it into the film) were conspicuously enchanted with his charisma and obvious gifts and oddly unaware of or unconcerned about his personal pain. Only the seasoned American Buddhist scholar in a fleeting interview respectfully suggested that Trungpa's death at age forty-six, largely due to alcoholism, was something to be lamented. He could have lived a much longer life, the scholar suggested, carrying his teachings further. But the camera seemed to drop the interview quickly, returning to the steady flow of awe-inspired praise.

Like other talented young Tibetan monks in the 1970s and '80s, Trungpa moved to the United States to introduce the Dharma (Buddhist teachings) to Western students. Because I know personally other senior Tibetan Buddhist teachers with comparable histories, I had heard about surreal transitions made to new countries, as if they'd landed on the moon without a space suit. And for most of these teachers, including Trungpa, such dramatic change came on the heels of a traumatic escape from their home country. I imagined that Trungpa might also have suffered the myriad ripple effects of culture shock, loss of loved ones, and perhaps even the discomforting feelings of fraudulence so common among his peers.

DEVELOPMENTAL STRUGGLES AMONG AMERICAN BUDDHISTS

As the documentary continued, I considered the possibility that American Buddhists (with some exceptions) have skipped the developmental stage that would allow us to more easily notice and respond to our teacher's subjectivity. Something has prevented us from understanding that even revered teachers have childhood memories in need of integration, unexpected personal loss, and addictions influenced by genetic predispositions requiring treatment beyond the spiritual realm. So too, teachers long for closeness with others, get lonely, and want friends who can tolerate and challenge their flawed humanness.

In short, we American Buddhists are struggling to mature. We still tend to function like children who idealize their caretakers in order to feel safely bonded to an all-powerful other. And while I recognize that these are sweeping claims, I nevertheless sense a pervasive struggle to develop the more adult capacity to contextualize our teachers and to recognize and make room for their participation in ordinary human experience.

There is a poignant irony at play in this struggle. As Buddhists, we are encouraged to be acutely aware of suffering, its causes and conditions. The Buddha Shakyamuni famously said that he had only one thing to teach—suffering and its end.[1] And yet, even in a Buddhist tradition predicated on devotion to one's teacher, we seem conspicuously uninterested in a beloved teacher's experience of suffering. Perhaps, in part, we have been so invested in the ameliorative power of our Buddhist practice that we have struggled to recognize the uniquely personal ways in which everyone, including senior Buddhists teachers, feel the endless manifestations of psychological pain by nature of being incarnate, chronically vulnerable, and usually without ready answers to our many nagging questions.

Some of these struggles, I recognize, are complicated by practices that encourage students to idealize their teachers as "fully realized." Tibetan Buddhist teachings especially suggest that it is only when we recognize the Buddhahood in our teachers that we receive the blessings of an awakened being. These teachings, which offer remarkable potential to expand our perceptual awareness, are nevertheless easily misappropriated in the service of splitting Buddhahood from personhood, teacher from self.

INTERSUBJECTIVITY AND PATTERNS OF ENGAGEMENT

As a relational psychoanalyst, I have spent much of my training and professional life exploring how relationships—to oneself, to culture, and to loved ones—develop. As a Buddhist, I've been similarly engaged in examining how we cultivate a deeper and more authentic sense of "inter-being" with one another. And as a Buddhist psychoanalyst, I've attempted to understand how these two disciplines might be mutually supportive in enhancing our efforts at meaningful and sustainable relationship.

With all this in mind, in the days after seeing *Crazy Wisdom* I found myself revisiting intersubjective theory and its insight into how we develop the ability to be seen and known and to see and know others. In contrast to classical Freudian theory, which emphasizes the baby's inner maelstrom of drives and fantasies regardless of the quality of parenting it receives, an intersubjective perspective shifts the focus to how babies develop a sense of self and other through relationship with a primary caretaker. The original intersubjective theorists (Atwood, Stolorow, Orange, Benjamin, etc.) sought to bring the locus of psychoanalytic attention to the particular ways in which a baby and his caretaker partake in "mutual patterns of engagement" in which, ideally, the baby is helped in regulating his experience of tension and emotionality.[2] These recurring patterns involve the many nuances of physical contact, how a baby is handled during feeding, bathing, play, and preparation for sleep.

Through this ongoing dance in everyday reality, the baby and caretaker may begin to experience a growing sense of attunement and, as a result, a bolstered trust that their fundamental needs, feelings, and intentions can be known to each other. It is, perhaps, another way of describing the feeling of being loved, of sensing that one's very personhood has elicited a deep and steadfast curiosity. One of the primary fruits of this mutual recognition is that slowly the baby begins to see that the mother has her own reality that can be discerned and related to, just as the baby has been known by his mother or mothering one. For the baby, it is a developmental achievement to step into the shoes of the caretaker, to some degree, just as the caretaker tries to do this for the child. This requires giving and getting a finely tuned attention. Such attunement is far more than just mutual influence. The process gives the baby psychic fuel for an ongoing sense that he can be known by others and he may come to know others. Jessica Benjamin notes that this intersubjective experience provides the basis for the feeling of being known in the other's view of us.[3] It is the process through which "we become able to grasp the other as having a separate yet similar mind."[4]

As this theory developed, the intersubjectivists began to describe the space that (ideally) develops between a baby and his caretaker, or for that matter, any two people, as "a third space." It is a quality of relatedness that grows out of a space in one's own mind housing our curiosity for what it feels like to be in relationship. It is a dynamic and generative space that allows something lively to grow between oneself and another.[5] Particularly relevant to Buddhism is the notion that such a space requires a temporary surrender of self and that through this surrender a young child is able to sustain connection to the caretaker's mind while more readily accepting his or her separateness and unique personhood.

For a variety of reasons, not every baby is cared for in such a way that permits this lively space to develop within his own mind and between the baby and his caretaker. If a parent is distracted, suffering from trauma or depression that has not been worked through, he or she may be unable to offer the baby the nuanced attunement it needs. Thus, when a third space never develops, or develops and breaks down, the child may feel that he lacks the agency to affect his caretaker. The child may feel merely done to and reactive, helplessly lost in the shadow of the other.[6]

Many adults see themselves reflected in the description of helplessness that ensues when the space of thirdness has been rendered too tenuous with their own caretakers. Who hasn't, at some point, suffered the experience of feeling done to, of being in a relationship with someone who seems strikingly uninterested in how we are responding, whether or not we're interested or nourished or engaged?

What is harder to see in oneself are the ways we may protect ourselves from a collapsed third space through feelings of omnipotence or omnipresence. Rather than suffer the feeling of being done to, we may opt to be the one who controls the collapsed space by reactively doing to others or by dominating a relational field through a disengaged musing. We may opt to make others feel helpless instead of being on the receiving end of their efforts at control and omnipotence. For the Buddhist student, this may take the form of disengaged self-reflection or a more depersonalized spiritual contemplation that makes it difficult for the teacher to see anything specific in the student's subjective experience.

## Imperfect Attunement

As good therapists from all schools of thought know intuitively, our ability to find and sustain interpersonal experience that is dynamic and lively does not come from having a history of perfect attunement. There is no such thing as two people—whether it is a baby and her mother, two lovers, or a teacher and student—who are perfectly in sync with each other's needs and wishes. Real intimacy arises from an ongoing process of connection that at some point is disrupted and then, ideally, repaired. I think of this as an interpersonal crochet stitch: connection, disruption, repair, over and over again, until a fabric is created with enough strength and flexibility to endure the wear of any two people attempting to know one another.

A "perfect match" is a compelling fantasy, however. When seeking romantic partners, we too often hold out for "the one" who knows, as if magically, just how to talk to us, touch us, comfort us without struggle or discord. When seeking therapists, patients so often hope to find that perfectly sage being who has transcended his or her own human struggle and can thus serve as a knower of all truths and who therefore knows just how to usher the patient toward wellness. And when seeking spiritual mentors, students are on the lookout for the enlightened being in their midst who glides graciously through life without struggle and who knows just how to usher the student toward awakening as quickly as possible.

This fantasy is motivated in part by a wish to have a world perfectly attuned to our own personhood. D. W. Winnicott suggested that if we are indeed blessed to begin our lives with some semblance of a world that *seems* perfectly attuned to us, we are more likely to have that magnificent experience of "going on being" in which we can simply rest in our being-ness without premature concern for those in our midst.[7] We get to recover from our arduous journey into this life and grow stronger as we prepare for the many challenges ahead.

Eventually, however, the child must recognize a much larger world apart from herself. Such a world is first experienced uncomfortably as "not-me," but eventually it becomes a rich and wondrous place replete with the joys of spontaneous discovery. The self psychologist Heinz Kohut suggested that the child makes this pivotal discovery through "optimal frustrations" in which perceived idealizations of the parent are slowly challenged, and the parent becomes in the child's eyes less Herculean and more human.[8] Such a child thus learns that other people have their own reality that the child cannot control, an otherness to be bumped up against and relied upon but not magically manipulated. A third space takes hold in the mind where even the young child becomes aware of relating to another person and that they are building a new space between them.

I think it is fair to suggest that many Westerners who seek out Buddhism as a spiritual path may have suffered early relational experiences that did not bolster a capacity to feel safely engaged with a world beyond their control. Having spent my entire adulthood and much of my childhood surrounded by Western Buddhists, it seems that relatively few arrive in Buddhist centers off the wings of psychic victory. Typically, practitioners have a psychologically complex history, often one heavily influenced by trauma or loss. Their spiritual efforts are made in the attempt to address difficult and vexing forms of psychological pain.

It is, in part, for this reason that I have been curious about the relationship between the Buddhist teacher and the student. In a dyad comparable to the psychoanalytic one, the teacher and student find themselves enacting their individual emotional histories. I believe that these enactments have contributed to the many examples we now have of boundary violations, students who have felt manipulated and even abused by their teachers, and teachers who have felt manipulated and abused by their students. From what I have observed, in most cases both participants have been vulnerable to their unconscious longing for perfect attunement, for a merger experience in which idealizations obscure a realistic view of an actual human being.

## SUFFERING OF BUDDHIST TEACHERS

Over the past twenty-five years, there has been increasing attention paid to the ways in which Buddhist students have suffered from teachers unconsciously seeking omnipotence and merger experience. But there has been a striking absence of interest in how teachers suffer when their students enact unconscious desires and longing. In much the same way psychoanalytic literature has placed a primary emphasis on the infant's experience with relatively little attention paid to the mother's subjectivity, her complex mosaic of needs and fears, Buddhist scholars have tended to privilege the person who seems more obviously vulnerable. It is tempting, particularly for the Western student, to ignore the reality that there are two sentient beings in this dyad and that both have psyches which render them vulnerable to the shadow side of human behavior. And when a student's (or researcher's) idealization of the teacher is operative, it becomes nearly impossible for them to hold in tension the teacher's gifts and his or her vulnerability.

In order for a teacher (or a parent or therapist for that matter) to frustrate the natural idealizations that arise, they need to have enough core self-esteem to tolerate being seen as less of a spiritual superhero and more of a flawed person with a mosaic of strengths and limitations like everyone else. If they are narcissistically wounded, however, they may encourage the idealizations and even treat the idealizing one as if he or she is a mere extension of themselves. Within the teacher/student dyad, Western students, especially with their greater candor, have the opportunity to offer as a gift to their teacher the ability to recognize and affirm the teacher's subjectivity. In doing so, they affirm that they too need a personal ego that is strong and supple enough to recover from and manage life's ongoing challenges.

All this to say it takes two to build a third space. If a teacher has some willingness to be seen as a whole being—in addition to having a kind heart and a liberated mind—he or she may welcome the student's increased efforts to withdraw idealizations and to work instead toward building up in themselves what they had been placing exclusively in the teacher.

Collectively, teachers and students alike pay a big price when this mutuality does not develop. Trungpa Rinpoche is not alone among famous spiritual teachers in having suffered from an addiction, perhaps fueled by personal and collective trauma, that required attention and treatment he never received. There are scores of senior Buddhist teachers (and I suspect this is true for all faith traditions) who privately suffer terrible pain that goes untreated. The world was shocked when Mother Theresa's letters were published attesting to her forty years of doubt and depression. What distressed me upon hearing of her letters was not that she had suffered depression—who hasn't?—but that she was unable to find help. Why was she left to manage such a long dark night of the soul alone?

I cannot know whether or not Trungpa had students who, out of feelings of concern, made efforts to respectfully confront him. I suspect there must have been many who were troubled by his relationship to alcohol and others who knew he suffered neglect from his adoring students in their selective inattention. I imagine that like most people in the throws of addiction, Trungpa would have resisted such concern. Whatever the case, it seems important to explore how Western Buddhist students might go about approaching their teacher's humanity and subjective struggles.

*** 

Having befriended a senior teacher in the Tibetan tradition, I am aware of my own struggles to create a roomier third space between us. My teacher, like Trungpa Rinpoche, has a fantastic sense of humor and playfulness. There are plenty of good laughs to be had when we reflect on the absurdity of our woeful human struggles. But as we all know, if we're looking to hide from a deeper, potentially more painful *and* healing exploration of these struggles, humor is a powerful defense. Trungpa knew how to play; it was one of his many obvious gifts. But the shadow side of this gift was that it camouflaged more serious matters that could not be healed through play alone.

I have had endless conversations with my teacher over the years in which I've been aware that something poignant or challenging has transpired in his life. In the past two years alone, two of his most devoted students died from sudden illness. These were thriving middle-aged men, people of great faith who had cared for our teacher and community for decades. After their passing, our teacher was called in by their respective families to tend to *their* suffering and to facilitate the practices utilized in death and dying in the Tibetan tradition.

On a few different occasions following these losses, I asked my teacher how he was feeling. In response, he tended to say, "How much are you going to charge me for this session?" I laughed. He was funny. We changed the subject. Eventually I mustered the courage to ask again. This time he dug his finger deep into his ear like a nervous boy, looked at the floor and said, "Truthfully, I feel numb." I nodded. He looked at me and we nodded together. I could see the raw sadness in his eyes as he held my gaze longer than usual. Then the phone rang and our conversation was over.

One year later, a senior monk and longtime friend of my teacher suffered a brain aneurism and fell into a coma for several weeks. We had all been together for a monthlong teaching only a few months prior. He'd been vital and energized, organizing a major event. Suddenly he was lying unresponsive in an ICU. My teacher left immediately to be with him, to say prayers and to support him and his family in any way he could.

When my teacher returned two weeks later, I asked him how he was doing. There was more ear exploration, more jokes. I was ready to give up. He scratched his shaved head with a long wooden back scratcher. He shook his head, staring at his computer, his cell phone, his desk. He looked like a fourteen-year-old boy with too few words to talk about his inner life. Then he stared at the floor.

"When this happens I think, 'Who's next?'"

For a fleeting moment we looked at each other. I added, "It's rough when the people you know and care about get sick. Makes you feel vulnerable."

He nodded, looked me dead in the eye and said, "How much is *that* going to cost me?" I told him it was going to be expensive. He should expect a hefty bill. We laughed, the phone rang, and he received a text; the conversation was over.

As I reflect on my own efforts to express concern for my teacher's well-being, I appreciate the complexity of this relationship and all relationships that involve contrasting backgrounds and cultural influences. My teacher, like Trungpa, comes from a world reinforced by his spiritual and monastic education, a world that emphasizes the freedom that can result from softening our grip on personal experience. And as anyone who has ever studied Buddhism knows, we taste liberation in seeing that our personal pain is merely an inroad to the shared experience of being human.

But this approach also has a shadow side. How can we increase our sensitivity toward and comfort with this shadow? We must recognize that our teachers need to be known as individuals, too. My hope is that slowly we may begin to actively build a space where our teachers can come into view, not only for their gifts of insight and compassion, but also in the fullness of their own human struggle and need for help. In this way, our teachers will also be granted the gift of looking into the eyes of a Buddha.

## NOTES

1. Quoted in F. L. Woodward, *Some Sayings of the Buddha* (London: Gordon Press, 1939), p. 294.

2. Jessica Benjamin, "Creating an Intersubjective Reality: Commentary on a Paper by Arnold Roths," *Psychoanalytic Dialogues* 15 (2005): 447–457.

3. *Ibid.*

4. Jessica Benjamin, "Beyond Doer and Done To: An Intersubjective View of Thirdness," *The Psychoanalytic Quarterly* 73 (2004): 5–46.

5. *Ibid.*

6. *Ibid.*

7. D. W. Winnicott, "Ego Integration in Child Development" (1962), in *The Maturational Processes and the Facilitating Environment* (New York: International Universities Press, 1965), p. 60.

8. Heinz Kohut, *The Analysis of the Self* (New York: International Universities Press, 1971), p. 64.

# BUDDHA AS A WALKAWAY

ALEXANDRA FIDYK

Just as the awakened ones of the past
Aroused an awakened mind
And progressively established themselves
In the practice of the Bodhisattva,
So I too for the benefit of beings
Shall arouse in an awakened mind
And progressively train myself in those practices.
            —Shantideva, *The Way of the Bodhisattva*

The study and practice of Zen Buddhism for many is a way to ease suffering. Mindfulness, compassion, impermanence, nonattachment, interdependence, and emptiness are some qualities of being with which one becomes familiar on this path. Mindfulness practice—sitting in *zazen*—hosts a conscious silence that envelops an inexpressible direct perception of the intangible, all-encompassing relational world in which all things are connected. This path most often cultivates insight as "no-self"—a state experienced as constant flux, ever related, ever changing. As insight into the self-in-process develops, one begins to see the humor in

Alexandra Fidyk, Ph.D., is an assistant professor on the Faculty of Education at the University of Alberta and adjunct faculty at Pacifica Graduate Institute. She is also a certified Jungian psychotherapist, trained as well in family constellation systems and integrated body psychodynamics.

an "I" that is fixed, separated from other, or from a world that does not breathe all sentient beings into and out of existence.

Often one comes to Buddhist and depth psychological practice with the same intention—to engage in individual development—whether or not the intention is known. In Buddhism one sits in meditation; one discovers the gifts of heightened awareness; one releases from attachment. In depth psychology one sits in analysis; one discovers shadow elements; one learns to withdraw projections. Either path is usually taken because of one's experiences of profound doubt, fear, despair, or loss. Certainly there is the Sangha, a community that teaches or meets for Dharma. There are Bodhisattvas who from compassion vow to alleviate the suffering of others. When engaged in meditation, one might partake in groups or retreats, even join others in a common human vulnerability. Yet one does not often think of coming to Buddhism as a way to develop or address group consciousness. The same is true in depth psychology. Most work is done with a therapist or analyst and often the work does not extend beyond this dyad. Emphasis is on the individual in relation to his or her suffering but not in relation to a collective.

### GROUPS AND SCAPEGOATING

Arthur Colman's *Up from Scapegoating*, an important text on awakening consciousness in groups, explores the nature of the boundary between an individual and a group without assuming, as is inherent within the depth psychological community, that the individual or individual consciousness is the central concern. Colman, a psychiatrist and Jungian analyst, writes:

> I am interested in exploring consciousness and the unconscious as both individual and group states, entertaining the idea that individuation is relevant to groups as well as to individuals and that the *critical relationship* between these two processes is manifested in the archetype of the scapegoat.[1]

Colman highlights a discriminating connection, a "juxtaposition," between the development in individuals and in groups in relation to individuation.[2] When a scapegoat exists, it not only hinders group development but also the process of individual shadow integration among group members. The focus of much Jungian therapy or analysis is on personal psychological development and not one's relationship to the collective, particularly the relationship between the individual shadow and the group scapegoat. By scapegoating, I mean identifying and blaming another for wrongdoing and "cast[ing them] out of the community in order to leave the remaining members with a feeling of guiltlessness, atoned (at-one) with the collective standards of behavior."[3] For Colman, "as long as there are scapegoats—unintegrated shadow figures for the group—integration of the shadow within the individual is an illusion."[4] "One might even say," he continues with emphasis, "that for the individual, the process of individuation will always be held hostage to the presence of the scapegoat in the larger community."[5] Conversely, group consciousness will also be kidnapped from its own authority and agency if the group is not awakened to its own separating tendencies.

The challenge then is to acknowledge a difference between self and other without separating them so schismatically that *no* relation at all is possible, a relation that is ever-present in the meta-mix of greater forces. Individuation requires acceptance of one's responsibility for suffering and scapegoating and a commitment to alleviate both, knowing that the consciousness of self and other is always interrelated and interdependent.

The concept of unity is a theme in all scapegoating activity, whether the context is biblical or political.[6] The scapegoat expresses and carries the group's urge toward "its own wholeness by excluding its disparate elements."[7] Scapegoating can exist anywhere there is "a transfer of negative attribution from one part of a system to another" or to another system in order to meet "what is perceived to be a unifying survival function for the system as a whole."[8] Within a group, the scapegoat is created by projecting the unacceptable side of group life elsewhere. "The guilt of society, is the guilt of order"; accordingly, "the guilty are those whose authority imposes [this] order."[9] The underbelly of that authority—"its relativity, its fragility, and its morality"—is revealed in the scapegoat.[10] From a Jungian perspective, the underbelly of the individual ego is called shadow and is projected onto others until it is accepted as one's own. For the group, common negative ground is a collective creation, a binding aspect of group identity, a "symbolic compromise for many individuals' negative projections."[11] So the scapegoat while not identical, is similar to the shadow in that it is "humanity's societal vessel for the shadow."[12]

Healthy individuation, from a Jungian view, includes respect for the integrated nature of our lives. Individuation demands that our bonds with others—human, animal, or vegetable—be included in the journey of our growth toward wholeness. We are all part of others' suffering, and we are all part of the scapegoating process. Our individual silence about scapegoating passively supports and supplies the shadow with more fuel, "defeating each of our attempts at integrating the archetype."[13] In order to accept responsibility for scapegoating, we must express our awareness and insights.

In the individual-group dynamic of scapegoating there are three kinds of participants: the scapegoat, the scapegoaters, and the walkaways. The scapegoat is the one (or ones) accused of causing misfortune and serves to relieve others of their responsibilities. The scapegoaters allocate blame to the scapegoat, shirking their own responsibilities thus strengthening their sense of power and righteousness. Walkaways are that subgroup "blessed [and] cursed" by the weight of sensitivity and an empathetic nature to the plight of the scapegoat. "They are 'called' to carry the [scapegoat] complex."[14] Some walkaways identify with the scapegoat and leave the group because they do not yet have enough ego strength to take up the hero's task—to overcome "the monster of darkness" or the "triumph of consciousness over the unconscious"; others take on the task of scapegoat hero but are ruled and destroyed by its energy.[15] The third way of the walkaway is shaman, healer, or teacher. This is the way of "the conscious scapegoat." These walkaways do not literally "walk away" but locate themselves on the margins of society, "one foot in the wilderness and the other in the town square."[16]

In such cases, the walkaway's stance is both a way of being and a way of knowing (ontological and epistemological presence). The walkaway must come to relate consciously to the meaning of the scapegoat. "[I]n this search and service is their healing."[17] As Colman puts it, this stance is "a comment and an attitude rather than a prescription."[18] From the perspective of Jungian analyst Sylvia Perera, it is through "conscious sacrifice of the inflated, collective identity as scapegoat and savior," that "these wounds can better be borne openly—suffered as open conflicts between the voice of the collective and the messages of the individual Self."[19] Through service and vulnerability, the walkaway, according to Jungian author Erich Neumann, reverses the act of scapegoating.

> In contrast to scapegoat psychology, in which the individual eliminates his own evil by projecting it onto the weaker brethren, we now find that the exact opposite is happening: we encounter the phenomenon of "vicarious suffering." The individual assumes personal responsibility for part of the burden of the collective, and he decontaminates this evil by integrating it into his own inner process of transformation. If the operation is successful, it leads to an inner liberation of the collective, which in part at least is redeemed from this evil.[20]

In such a situation, the walkaway draws energy from the Wise One archetype, dwelling as hyphen between individual and group consciousness. She or he "makes it possible to honor the dual reality of individual and group member" and acts so to unlock the unconscious contagion underlying the scapegoat dynamic.[21] Though the walkaway's response to scapegoating seems subjective, when it is complete and wise that service includes the decision to return to the community consciously and deliberately. From this understanding of the relational bond between scapegoat and scapegoaters, I reread the life of Buddha as a walkaway.

## Siddhartha Gautama as Walkaway

While there are conflicting details among epic poems, oral history, and written accounts of the biography of Siddhartha Gautama, I want to provide a simple account of his life in order to explore his ethical choice within the scapegoat dynamic. Born in about 563 B.C., Siddhartha was the son of Śuddhodana, a Raja chieftain in the Sakya clan of the Kshatriya (warrior) caste. His mother's name was Maya. Gautama was the family name. Some versions say his mother died when he was born and he was then raised by her youngest sister. Siddhartha (Pali: Siddhattha, means "he who achieves his aim") nevertheless lived a sheltered life within the confines of his family's estate. Some sources claim that he was destined at birth to live the life of a prince and had three palaces built for his seasonal residence. More recent scholarship doubts this status, proposing that his father, wishing for him to be a great king, shielded Siddhartha from religious teachings and knowledge of human suffering. At sixteen Siddhartha was said to have entered into an arranged marriage to his cousin who was the same age. For years thereafter Siddhartha was provided for by his father and protected from the larger world until his wife gave birth to their only son when Siddhartha was about 29.

At that time, Siddhartha objected to his father's dictates and left the protective confines of the family estate. The most popular legend states,

> Despite his father's efforts . . . Siddhartha was said to have seen an old man. When his charioteer Channa explained to him that all people grew old, the prince went on further trips beyond the palace. On these he encountered a diseased man, a decaying corpse, and an ascetic. These depressed him and he initially strove to overcome ageing, sickness and death by living the life of an ascetic.[22]

Moved by such suffering, one night Siddhartha walked away from his privileged life. So began his wandering and studying as an ascetic, begging for alms in the street. His practice continued under the tutelage of two hermit masters with whom he learned quickly how to achieve high levels of meditative consciousness. Each sage asked Siddhartha to succeed him; he refused both and moved on to learn more.

Along with a small group of companions, Siddhartha Gautama sought liberation through deprivation of comforts, clothes, and food. After nearly starving to death, Siddhartha recognized the value of the physical body for awakening. Remembering how, as a child of about seven, he had fallen into a pleasant heightened awareness while watching his father attending the crops, he took to sitting in a concentrated and focused state, *jhāna*. From this practice, which required a healthy physical body and a balanced mind, Siddhartha discovered the Middle Way—a path of moderation between the extremes of self-deprivation and self-indulgence. While sitting under the Bodhi (pipal) tree, in such a practice, he vowed to remain there till he had found truth. After an indeterminate amount of time—a few or several days—Siddhartha awoke to the deep radiance of reality and from then on he was known as the Buddha or "Awakened One."

In his awakening, he saw clearly into the cause of and release from *dukkha*—truths he taught soon after his awakening, as the Four Noble Truths. *Dukkha* refers to a quality of experience, an off-centered or diseased state, like a wheel off its axle or a bone out of its socket. The First Noble Truth teaches that *dukkha* exists. The Second Noble Truth tells that *dukkha* arises because one clings to or craves particular states, things, outcomes. The Third Noble Truth describes an alternative to *dukkha* which is not clinging to one's desires for particular states, things, outcomes. The Fourth Noble Truth presents the path to end *dukkha* through eight practices: right speech, right action, right livelihood (ethics, *sila*), right effort, right awareness, right concentration (mindfulness, Samadhi), right thought, and right understanding (wisdom, *prajna*, which also includes previous two). In this context, "right" means "in the right way," "straight," not bent or crooked. The "right" way arises from love and compassion (*metta*) to benefit both self and other. For example, right livelihood signifies work that, like right action, does not result in intentional harm to others, including ecological systems and animals.[23]

According to many stories, immediately after his awakening, the Buddha debated whether or not he should teach the Dharma to others. He doubted if others who were consumed by their own righteousness or ignorance could recognize and commit to the path. It is a profound and subtle way, taking years of practice, and demands discipline, courage, strength, and readiness. After he had achieved a profound awakening, the Buddha had the option to remain in nondual consciousness or return to an ordinary albeit awakened state and serve the collective.

Gautama chose to teach and become a walkaway who served himself and the group from a place of Samadhi. For the remaining forty-five years of his life, he traveled across what is now northern India and southern Nepal, teaching a vast range of people. With the profound knowledge that he and all others arose together as a unity within a context, he was of service to both his individuation and the liberation of others from *dukkha*.

In the Buddha's enlightenment, he clearly saw the nature of reality as an interconnected web where each of us is a participant in what is and what unfolds—an interdependent relationship with everything in and around us. The unity and interrelationship of all phenomena and the intrinsically dynamic nature of the universe can be experienced in the body through simple meditation, *bhavana*, which best translates as "mental development."[24] For both animate and inanimate entities, life is inescapably connected and extends beyond the boundaries of our skin. We codependently arise with all entities in the universe; we are inter-beings.[25] Jung called this *unus mundus* or interconnected dependency. Indeed, part of the very healing process is to see one's story, one's suffering, as part of the human narrative forever embedded in a living, breathing cosmos. This concept of wholeness means that our potential as humans is a unifying principle of our species. How then does one stand up from meditation and partake in service?

## Concluding Remarks

The same can be asked of therapists and analysts: How does our work with patients contribute to the well-being of all beings? In our analytical groups and organizations, we have behaved in fractious and notoriously scapegoating ways. Colman seems well positioned to alert the professional body to the projective contagion which functions unconsciously wherever psychotherapeutically and analytically trained people gather. Depth psychological groups are often isolated within their own communities and tend to work in a segregated style. Can we return from our individuation quest with knowledge *for* the group and an understanding of how the stress within the self-group continuum initially contributed to the quest? It is only within the relationship to others that one experiences conflict and dis-ease which might direct one into analysis or to Buddhist practice. It is too easy to stay on the margins, and perhaps equally easy to remain at the center without any critique of the workings and projections of the group. Striking a balance means that one has a responsibility to understand the group unconscious—an ethical commitment to both task and process—which serves both the individual and the collective psyche. As Colman suggests:

> only through detailed experiential knowledge of the collective
> unconscious of the group, such as we have worked toward in
> the individual and within the therapeutic dyad, can we guard

against its destructiveness and learn to establish more appropriate conditions for a nurturing relationship between group and individual.[26]

The path recommended is that of a teacher or walkaway who never really leaves: one who must undergo her or his own transformation through descent and conscious return, choosing to become critically engaged in the dynamics of various collectives. The teacher thus remains aware of his or her own role in creating and accepting the very scapegoating he or she abhors.[27] In this way, we wake up to our own projections and work individually and collectively to integrate that which was previously projected and scapegoated. The walkaway unites that which was earlier separated, seeing the other as self, and insists on hosting all ten thousand beings.

## NOTES

1. Arthur D. Colman, *Up from Scapegoating: Awakening Consciousness in Groups* (Wilmette, IL: Chiron, 1995), p. xvi, my italics.

2. *Ibid.*, p. 5.

3. Sylvia Brinton Perera, *The Scapegoat Complex: Toward a Mythology of Shadow and Guilt* (Toronto: Inner City Books, 1986), p. 9.

4. Colman, *Up from Scapegoating*, p. 5.

5. *Ibid.*

6. Richard Kearney, *Strangers, Gods and Monsters: Interpreting Otherness* (London: Routledge, 2002).

7. Colman, *Up from Scapegoating*, p. 7.

8. *Ibid.*

9. Jacob Brownowski, "The Scapegoat King," in *The Scapegoat: Ritual and Literature,* edited by John B. Vickery and J'nan M. Sellery (Boston: Houghton Mifflin Co., 1972), p. 37.

10. René Girard, *The Scapegoat*, trans. Yvonne Freccero (Baltimore: Johns Hopkins University Press, 1986), p. 21.

11. Colman, *Up from Scapegoating*, p. 7.

12. *Ibid.* It is important to remember that originally the scapegoat was an animal or human chosen for sacrifice to the underworld god to appease his anger and to heal the community.

This sacrificial strategy furnished communities with a binding identity, with a basic sense of who is included and who is excluded. As such the scapegoat was a healing agent; it functioned to invite the transpersonal dimension to renew the community which saw itself as embedded in and dependent on unknown forces. Scapegoat rituals were used "to enrich meaning or call attention to other levels of existence. . . . [They] incorporate[d] evil and death along with life and goodness into a single, grand, unifying pattern." As such, one's identity was personal, communal, *and* transpersonal. Because of this collective forgetting and a desire to avert catastrophe, the scapegoat ritual has become trivialized, and its deeper meaning remains unconscious. There then is a dangerous tendency to blame certain people or groups, often ethnic and cultural minorities, for the "evil" in the world, particularly since "God" and those who identify with his image (dominant groups, the right, fundamentalists, etc.) see themselves as only good; thus, the adverse must be cast elsewhere. Mary Douglas, *Purity and Danger: An Analysis of Concepts of Pollution and Taboo* (London: Routledge and Kegan Paul, 1966), p. 53.

13. Colman, *Up from Scapegoating*, p. 10.

14. Perera, *The Scapegoat Complex*, p. 98.

15. C. G. Jung, "The Psychology of the Child Archetype," in *The Archetypes and the Collective Unconscious*, vol. 9i, *The Collected Works of C. G. Jung* (Princeton, NJ: Princeton University Press, 1959), § 284.

16. Colman, *Up from Scapegoating*, p. 18.

17. Perera, *The Scapegoat Complex*, p. 98.

18. Colman, *Up from Scapegoating*, p. 18.

19. Perera, *The Scapegoat Complex*, p. 98.

20. Erich Neumann, *Depth Psychology and a New Ethic*, trans. Eugene Rolfe (Boston: Shambhala Publications, 1990), p. 130.

21. Colman, *Up from Scapegoating*, p. 18.

22. "Gautama Buddha," accessed April 11, 2013, at http://en.wikipedia.org/wiki/Gautama_Buddha.

23. Alexandra Fidyk, "Suffering Within: Seven Moments of Ignorance," in *Epistemologies of Ignorance in Education*, edited by Eric Malewski and Nathalia Jaramillo (Charlotte, NC: Information Age Publishing, 2011), pp. 135–136.

24. Mark Epstein, *Thoughts without a Thinker: Psychotherapy from a Buddhist Perspective* (New York: Basic Books, 1996), p. 195.

25. Thich Nhat Hanh, *Peace in Every Step* (New York: Bantam, 1992).

26. *Ibid.*, p. 19.

27. *Ibid.*

# Humor, Healing, and Helping

# A Sense of Humor, Enlightenment, and Individuation

## DEON VAN ZYL

B ankei Yōtaku (1622–1693), an early popularizer of Zen, argues that the way to nondualist wisdom is to allow yourself to be surprised: "when you see and hear things that you hadn't originally anticipated seeing or hearing, it's through the dynamic function of the Buddha Mind that every one of you has."[1] The Buddha Mind, and enlightenment, are characterized by "waking up," consenting to being pleasantly surprised, opening to the present and finding joy in the ever-changing flow. All of these may be regarded as aspects of realizing the impermanence of life. In this mode of perceiving, there is no reification of a patterned viewpoint. Phenomena and experience are not solidified but seen in their relatedness to an ever-renewing context with a brand-new view of things.

Deon van Zyl, D.Phil., is a clinical psychologist and corporate consultant in private practice in Johannesburg, South Africa, and formerly associate professor of psychology at the University of Pretoria. He is a regular meditator in the Buddhist mindfulness tradition and author of "Polarity Processing: Self/No-Self, the Transcendent Function, and Wholeness" in *Self and No-Self* (2009). He publishes regular articles in *Mantis*, the journal of the South African Association of Jungian Analysts, most recently "The Clown Archetype: Reflections on the Age-Old Wisdom Within the Fool's Humour" (2007), "Holographic Dreaming" (2011), and "Vocation as Archetype—Instinctual Calling" (2013). His website is www.dvanzyl.co.za.

A moment of humor shares in the features of awakening. When we smile or laugh at something funny, we allow ourselves for a fleeting instant to take in something unexpected, new, and pleasantly surprising. In humor we are receptive and absorbed in the present moment. The mind is flexible, fluid, and not adhered to a fixed perspective. The mutability of humor comes close to the Buddhist notion of nonattachment, including the perception and experience of impermanence, albeit briefly. Even the etymology of the word *humor* is intrinsically linked to *fluid*, depicting its flexible, flowing, unaffixed, and transient nature. This malleable and effervescent way of seeing that is found in humor and other forms of awakening is also a core aspect of the theory and practice of depth psychology. From a Jungian point of view, the Self, which is the beginning and end of all our striving toward what Jung termed *individuation*, is "not just a static quantity or constant form, but is also a dynamic process . . . in a continually repeated process of rejuvenation."[2] Hermes from Greek mythology, Mercurius from Roman mythology, and the philosopher's stone from alchemy are symbolic depictions of this Self. Both Hermes and Mercurius are many-sided, changeable, and shape-shifting, very much like the liquid element of Mercury or quicksilver. Mercury is solid and liquid: it flows and fits into the shape or context in which it finds itself. In this sense it shares its "aquaeositas" with water and all the qualities that water possesses.[3] Similarly, the philosopher's stone is not a fixed entity with solidity and permanence but growing and living, with rejuvenating properties. It is very much akin to liquid and water, almost a "rotating aquasphere."[4]

A genuine experience of Self would therefore entail elements of flow, flexibility, change, release of attachment to a fixed viewpoint, and openness to surprise. Indeed, Jung emphasized that the end goal of analysis is a state of fluidity:

> My aim is to bring about a psychic state in which my patient
> begins to experiment with his own nature—a state of fluidity,
> change, and growth where nothing is eternally fixed and
> hopelessly petrified.[5]

Awakening, from a Buddhist point of view, and individuation, from a depth psychological perspective, both entail a nonattached and pliable realization of the impermanence of things and of life's continuous flow. The surprise aspect of humor can make a significant contribution to this realization and therefore support the journey toward enlightenment and individuation. Although the release of a fixed viewpoint during a humorous moment is short-lived, the cultivation of a regular sense of humor provides more opportunities to experience openings that may ultimately awaken a new and fresh view of the world.

HUMOROUS AMBIGUITY, NO-SELF, AND THE TRANSCENDENT FUNCTION

Consider these notices that appeared in a church bulletin:

> *This afternoon there will be meetings in the north and south ends of the church. Children will be baptized on both ends.*

> *Thursday at 8 p.m. there will be a meeting of the Little Mothers Club. All those wishing to become Little Mothers will please meet the Minister in his study.*

The unexpected surprise is suddenly to see the "other side" of the baby being baptized, or the "other side" of the minister in his study. We have to release our usual expectations. We become fleetingly unattached to our views and then our vantage points can change.

In addition to the surprise of humor, we experience the simultaneous presence of contrasting opposites and their incongruity. When the lofty and the profane meet—baptism and children's butts, religious morality and indecent procreation—the lofty is brought down to earth at the same time as the earthy is elevated to a higher status. For a moment before we smile or laugh, we are aware of contrast. The opposing poles don't belong together, but they are in one picture, inseparable and interacting. Although the two sides cannot be reconciled, they exist together, and this makes us smile or laugh.

During a humorous moment, it is as if each of the opposites becomes present, stands out clearly for what it is, and then disappears, becomes absent, and makes room for the presence of its opposite. This reminds me of the Buddha's famous formulation:

> When this is, that is;
> This arising, that arises;
> When this is not, that is not;
> This ceasing, that ceases.[6]

With reference to the church bulletin announcements, we can say:

> When sacred is, profane is;
> Sacred arising, profane arises;
> When sacredness is not, profanity is not;
> Sacredness ceasing, profanity ceases.

The opposites simultaneously emerge and recede. They are held and released and alternate in such a way that they become not either/ or but both/and. The sacred side of the polarity owes its existence to the profane and vice versa: we cannot know the one without the other. Each side is devoid of an inherent existence and is dependent on the other side for its own demarcation. Each opposite is a foundation for the other, each seeding the other. To use a Buddhist notion, they arise interdependently and have no-thingness of their own. As the renowned Buddhist philosopher Nāgārjuna said, "All the pairs are explained as being devoid of inherent existence because they originate in mutual dependence."[7] Jung alluded to this condition in his *Seven Sermons to the Dead*, where he said that the pairs of opposites do not exist because they cancel each other out.[8]

During a humorous moment we allow ourselves to perceive and experience the interdependent aspect of reality. We see that ideas, concepts, qualities, and experiences are empty of their own inherent existence. They have no independent and enduring substantial essence, but are interrelated and dependently connected. This way of seeing things is aptly described in Buddhism as "right view" and is the foundation of the Buddhist Noble Eightfold Path. This view is expressed in the terms *anatta* in Pali or *anatman* in Sanskrit, meaning "not-self" or "no-self." If humor can assist us with this kind of right view, then we may experience "a little bit of enlightenment" during a comical moment.[9] A more regular sense of humor, with an ongoing open attitude, can contribute significantly to the cultivation of the interdependent perspective while walking the Noble Eightfold Path.

From a Jungian point of view, we activate what Jung called the transcendent function when we open a dialogue between two poles of a conflict and allow a new position to emerge that is neither a combination of nor a rejection of the two.[10] Activating the transcendent function undergirds individuation and is the objective of Jungian analysis and human maturity. Humor, I believe, with its inherent embrace of opposites and subsequent altered perspective, is a form of transcendent function and has a definite role to play in the realization of Jung's notion of individuation.

Young-Eisendrath describes individuation as "the recognition and acceptance of the centre or the balancing of a dialectical system of 'self.'"[11] With humor you take a middle or central position between extremes and embrace the dialectical exchange between the opposites, playfully balancing both sides by giving them their equal due. The dialectical system of the Jungian view of Self is the dynamic liquid process that we referred to earlier, but its dialectical nature is also described in terms like *complexio oppositorum*, paradoxical, and antinomial.[12] According to Jung, this is why the alchemists were so fond of paradoxes when attempting to describe the *prima materia* (a symbol of self). The alchemists tried not only to "visualize the opposites together but to express them in the same breath."[13] This conjoined view is what is required to attain the acceptance of the center and the balancing of a dialectical system to which Young-Eisendrath refers. Humor is filled with paradox and plays a significant part in the process of individuation through participating in this balancing of a dialectical system of Self.

Jung claims,

> The shuttling to and fro of arguments and affects represents the transcendent function of opposites. The confrontation of the two positions generates a tension charged with energy and creates a living, third thing . . . that leads to a new level of being, a new situation. The transcendent function manifests itself as a quality of conjoined opposites.[14]

I propose that a humorous insight contains this "third thing" and a "new level of being" that emerges from the joining of opposites. You release a one-sided fixed view, allow the experience of its opposite, and bring both together in a view beyond the constraints of either/or. The opposites are both affirmed and negated and a new combination emerges which takes you to new facets of experience. When you play with the ambiguity that is inherent in a humorous moment you move into a different dimension that is delightful, captivating, and enchanting.

Jungian analyst Steven Joseph prefers the process phrase "transcendent functioning" to Jung's transcendent function and says it "involves at its core a letting go of fixed structures and identities."[15]

One can see that the fluid nature of humor enables new perspectives to emerge from the interplay between opposites and that a unifying or transcendent process makes this possible. Perhaps the Jungian notion of Self as the "ambivalent bridge" that unites the opposites in such a way that they can function together is exactly the dynamic process that makes it possible for humor to be the mediator between opposing aspects of experience.[16]

The constructivist perspective in depth psychology views Self as "an organising tendency arising in a situational context."[17] If the context requires some form of correction, a coordinating or balancing imperative, then the Self surfaces. Humor often emerges in contexts where there is rigidity or one-sidedness, such as authoritarian rule. Satirists, humorists, cartoonists, and clowns, like the court jesters of old, attempt to restore momentary balance in the way the psyche processes inbalance, either by amplifying the one-sidedness or by showing the exact opposite viewpoint. Clowning and humor, a two-sided or multisided view, are the antidote to unambiguity and unilateral attachment. In this way humor shares in the organizing tendency of the Self.

### Paradoxes, Koans, Jokes, and Nondual Wisdom

In the Buddhist tradition, haiku verses and koans are filled with surprises, paradoxical plays, and contrasting opposites. They often have the basic design of a joke and frequently one's first response is to smile. Here is a haiku by Demaru:

> Sitting like the Buddha,
> But bitten by mosquitoes
> In my Nirvāna.[18]

To manage the huge difference between nirvana and a mosquito bite one smiles. There is a momentary enfoldment of both extremes and a paradoxical playing with opposites in one picture. This moment of merging of contrast can also bring a bigger perspective, a nondualist insight with an element of wisdom. After all, where else can nirvana be realized but in and through samsara (the world of birth, death, and suffering)? Like everything else, nirvana and samsara are also codependent. Nirvana is a nonattached view of samsara and cannot be achieved without it. They are so inextricably linked that Nāgārjuna, in his renowned *Mūlamadhyamakakārikā*, says: "There is not even the slightest of difference between them."[19]

Koans and humor can work hand in hand to bring wisdom and teach enlightenment and are often used in Zen Buddhism for this purpose.

> Yanyang Shanxin asked Zhaozhou Congshen, "If I come with nothing, what then?" "Let it go!" replied Zhaozhou. "But I've come with nothing," answered Yanyang. "How can I let it go?" "Then go on carrying it!" said Zhaozhou. At this Yanyang was deeply enlightened.[20]

Koans like this elicit exactly the same sequence of thought process that Freud described with jokes: first "bafflement" and then "light dawning."[21] With koans and jokes the mind would first go "what?" and then "oh, yes, I see!" This process happens without rational prompting of insights. Koans and jokes are characterized by their economy in the way they trigger a new perspective. Freud emphasized the brevity of jokes and witticism, that they say things by not saying them.[22] This applies equally to koans. Freud sounds Zenlike when he describes that moment before the "bright idea" of a joke dawns: "One senses something rather undefinable, which I would best compare with an *absence*, a sudden letting-go of intellectual tension."[23]

In the end, the thriftiness, surprise, and paradox that are found in koans and jokes compel a different view, a shake-up of fixed perspectives. Zen teacher John Tarrant mentions the well-known joke about Sherlock Holmes and Dr. Watson as a case in point:

> They wake up in the middle of the night and Holmes says, "Watson, what do the stars make you think of?" "Well Holmes, I suppose I think of infinity, of the mysterious beauty of the universe, and of how much there is to discover. What do they make you think of?" "Well Watson, they make me think that someone has stolen our tent."[24]

While Holmes learns about the splendor of the universe, Watson is brought down to earth. As we smile at the surprising contrast, we also might just gain a modicum of insight and wisdom into the clash of conditions in everyday life. How about the following as a modern-day koan?

> Two politicians accuse each other of lying.
> Both are telling the truth.

When we are too precise, we lose our sense of humor and eventually our wisdom. When we are unequivocal about a rule, a procedure, an idea, a way of life, our own identity, we tend to cling to it, to fix it in permanence, and this is not funny. Holding on leaves no room for maneuvering or for a different viewpoint. By playfully stepping out of unyielding structure, humor helps with release, lightness, and freedom and contributes to a nondual perspective.

### CONCLUSION

Two of the important components of humor—surprise and embrace of ambiguity—can contribute significantly to the process of awakening and individuation. Surprise signifies a nonattached view from a Buddhist perspective. It brings recognition of impermanence with fluidity and an openness to the present moment. Humorous surprise can cultivate a sense of change, flow, flexibility, and rejuvenation, thereby matching the dynamics of the Jungian Self and the continual process of personal growth and rejuvenation.

The playful embrace of ambiguity during humor brings an awareness of interdependence and the accompanying insight that ideas, concepts, qualities, experiences, and things are empty of their own separate existence. This aspect of humor cultivates a Buddhist no-self and nondual viewpoint. When opposites are paradoxically visualized together in the same picture or event, humor is an expression of—and a contributor to—a transcendent functioning and a balancing of a dialectical system of Self. Humor can also bring momentary correction and equilibrium in the psyche within a context that is disproportionate and unbalanced. In this way it participates in the organizing tendency of the Self.

Finally, let's not forget that if the context of the humorous event is playful and safe, and the intention convivial, then being pleasantly surprised by paradoxical polarities can generate a pleasant feeling of mirth, cheerfulness, and even happiness. This kind of joy is not to be underrated as a core aspiration of all human beings.

## NOTES

1. Peter Haskel, trans., *Bankei Zen* (New York: Grove Press, 1984), p. 34, quoted in Ryūichi Abé and Peter Haskel, trans., *Great Fool, Zen Master Ryōkan: Poems, Letters, and other Writings* (Honolulu: University of Hawai'i Press, 1996), p. 56.

2. C. G. Jung, "The Structure and Dynamics of the Self," in *The Collected Works of C. G. Jung*, vol. 9ii, *Aion* (1959; repr., London: Routledge and Kegan Paul, 1970), § 411.

3. C. G. Jung, "The Conjunction," in *The Collected Works of C. G. Jung*, vol. 14, *Mysterium Coniunctionis* (1963; repr., London: Routledge and Kegan Paul, 1970), § 717.

4. C. G. Jung, "The Prima Materia," in *The Collected Works of C. G. Jung*, vol. 12, *Psychology and Alchemy* (1953; revised, London: Routledge and Kegan Paul, 1968), § 433.

5. C. G. Jung, "The Aims of Psychotherapy," in *The Collected Works of C. G. Jung*, vol. 16, *The Practice of Psychotherapy* (1954; repr., London: Routledge and Kegan Paul, 1970), § 99.

6. Quoted in J. Marvin Spiegelman and Mokusen Miyuki, *Buddhism and Jungian Psychology* (New Delhi: New Age Books, 2004), p. 131.

7. David Ross Komito, trans., *Nāgārjunas's Seventy Stanzas: A Buddhist Psychology of Emptiness* (New York: Snow Lion Publications, 1987), p. 138.

8. C. G. Jung, *The Red Book: Liber Novus*, ed. Sonu Shamdasani (London: W.W. Norton, 2009), p. 347–348.

9. Jack Engler, "Being Somebody and Being Nobody: A Reexamination of the Understanding of Self in Psychoanalysis and Buddhism," in Jeremy D. Safran, *Psychoanalysis and Buddhism: An Unfolding Dialogue* (Boston: Wisdom Publications, 2003), p. 41.

10. Jeffrey C. Miller, *The Transcendent Function: Jung's Model of Psychological Growth through Dialogue with the Unconscious* (New York: State University of New York Press, 2004).

11. Polly Young-Eisendrath and James Hall, *Jung's Self Psychology: A Constructivist Perspective* (New York: The Guilford Press, 1991), p. 39.

12. Jung, "The Structure and Dynamics of the Self," § 355.

13. Jung, "The Conjunction," § 36.

14. C. G. Jung, "The Transcendent Function," in *The Collected Works of C. G. Jung*, vol. 8, *The Structure and Dynamics of the Psyche* (1960; repr., London: Routledge and Kegan Paul, 1972), § 189.

15. Steven M. Joseph, "Presence and Absence through the Mirror of Transference: A Model of the Transcendent Function," *Journal of Analytical Psychology*, 42 (1): 150.

16. Quoted in Miller, *The Transcendent Function*, p. 71.

17. Young-Eisendrath and Hall, *Jung's Self Psychology*, p. 168.

18. Conrad Hyers, "The Smile of Truth," *Parabola: The Magazine of Myth and Tradition*, 12 (4): 51.

19. Jay L. Garfield, trans., *The Fundamental Wisdom of the Middle Way: Nāgārjuna's Mūlamadhyamakakārikā* (New York: Oxford University Press, 1995), p. 331.

20. Thomas Yūhō Kirchner, trans., *Entangling Vines: Zen Koans of the Shūmon Kattōshū* (Kyoto: Tenryu-Ji Institute for Philosophy and Religion, 2004), p. 5.

21. Sigmund Freud, *The Joke and Its Relation to the Unconscious*, trans. Joyce Crick (London: Penguin Books, 2002), Kindle Version, Section A, Analytic Part I Introduction, 12th paragraph.

22. Freud, *The Joke and Its Relation to the Unconscious*, Section A, Analytic Part I Introduction, 15th paragraph.

23. Freud, *The Joke and Its Relation to the Unconscious*, Section C, Theoretical Part VI The Relation of the Joke to Dreams and to the Unconscious, 15th paragraph—Freud's italic emphasis.

24. John Tarrant, "Paradox, Breakthrough and the Zen Koan," *Shift: At the Frontiers of Consciousness*, no. 6 (March-May 2005), p. 27.

# Reflections on Genjokoan, Kintsugi, and *Participation Mystique*
## Mutual Transformation through Shared Brokenness

MELVIN E. MILLER

Ring the bells that still can ring
Forget your perfect offering
There is a crack, a crack in everything
That's how the light gets in.
　　　　　　　　　—Leonard Cohen, "Anthem"

Melvin E. Miller, Ph.D., is a clinical psychologist and psychoanalyst and Charles A. Dana Professor of Psychology and director of doctoral training at Norwich University. He has conducted research and published in psychoanalysis and spiritual development and is past president of the Vermont Association for Psychoanalytic Studies and the Society for Research in Adult Development. He is on the faculty and a supervisor for the Vermont Institute for the Psychotherapies. He coedited, with P. Young-Eisendrath, *The Psychology of Mature Spirituality* (2000) and most recently, with D. Mathers and O. Ando, *Self and No-Self: Continuing the Dialogue between Buddhism and Psychotherapy* (2009). He has a private psychoanalytic practice in Montpelier, Vermont.

Heeding unformulated mental stirrings and paying close attention to nascent thoughts that percolate up from somewhere beneath everyday awareness are habits that I have practiced for years. Sometimes this openness leads to agreeable mental states. Occasionally it contributes to equanimity, but sometimes this practice gets me into trouble. Approaching the project at hand in such an unformulated manner was both exciting and distressing. What would I write about? What would I take on? Eventually, a few possibilities surfaced, but none that were particularly compelling. So I set it all aside for a while.

After a lengthy period, two curious words began to surface in tandem: *Genjokoan* and *kintsugi*. The first refers to a ready-made "life koan" and the second is a Japanese term for a special way of mending pottery. They felt like a pair of unwanted intruders with little in common. I'd shove them away, but they kept reappearing: *Genjokoan* and *kintsugi*. What is this about, I wondered? Why do I keep resisting them? Why do I treat them as if they were impetuous demons sent from some mythological underworld? Why are these words appearing at all, let alone together? Eventually, my resistance softened. I opened the door to them, though not without considerable reservations.

## GENJOKOAN

Upon reflection, I realized that I first heard the term *Genjokoan* a few years ago while listening to a talk by Shinzen Young, a Buddhist teacher.[1] Young described the Genjokoan as representing the core psychological conflict or dilemma that a person grapples with in life. It is one's "ready-made" or "custom-made" life conundrum. Young claimed that by working primarily on this core issue in one's formal practice and in ordinary walking-around existence, practices would deepen and lives would be transformed. The ready-made core issue *is* the work of a lifetime. He said there is really no other way to change a life. If we try to avoid the challenge of Genjokoan, it will perpetually return. What a fascinating notion. As a practicing psychoanalyst, this idea had immediate appeal, since I saw the truth of it manifested each day in the consulting room. Patients need to work over the same old issues. In analytic practice there is an axiom that is virtually inviolate:

the more painful the early trauma or wound, "the more likely it is to be woven into something we find ourselves compulsively repeating."[2] To be sure, each patient has a lifelong ready-made problem that keeps being revisited. In this respect, I saw the Genjokoan as the Buddhist version of the repetition compulsion and became excited by this point of apparent convergence.

In the autumn of 1233, at the age of thirty-two, Zen Master Eihei Dōgen wrote the Genjokoan that became the first chapter of his *Shobogenzo*, the book outlining the fundamental philosophy of Zen Buddhism.[3] After exploring a variety of sources, I found that this koan seemed more complex than what was suggested by Young's talks or by reducing Genjokoan to a version of the repetition compulsion. Dōgen wrote not only of the need to address the repetitive challenges of everyday life (one's custom-made koan), but of the necessity to recognize the entire phenomenal world as the Genjokoan. The "subjective realm and the objective realm, [all mental and all physical phenomena] the self and all things in the universe" are the Genjokoan.[4] Dōgen also meant that "the whole phenomenal world is entirely oneself."[5] The Genjokoan, therefore, is the path to understanding all of existence and its interconnectedness, the universal and the particular. Resolution of this koan, according to Dōgen, leads to awakening. Dairyu Wenger, a *Shobogenzo* scholar, noted that the term *Genjokoan* has been translated many ways, including: "the question of everyday life, actualizing the fundamental point, the matter at hand," definitions similar to those offered in Young's teachings.[6] But, in the same sentence, he describes Genjokoan as "the realized law of the universe, manifesting absolute reality, the actualization of enlightenment, [and] manifesting suchness."[7] The universal and the personal are one and the same. When you work on one, you are working on the other. An intriguing line in the Genjokoan reads, *"To study Buddhism is to study ourselves,"* which Zen teacher Shunryu Suzuki expanded into "to study ourselves is to study everything."[8] And, perhaps in an attempt to make this life project a little less daunting, Suzuki claims, "It is enough if you do one thing with sincerity. That is enough."[9] Again, this seems to bring us back to Young's notion of working on our own ready-made conundrum, trying to be as true to it—and ourselves—as we can be.

### Kintsugi

*Kintsugi* is a five-hundred-year-old practice of mending pottery with gold leaf. The term actually translates into something like "golden joinery"; it is the Japanese practice of repairing ceramic with gold-laced lacquer to illuminate the breakage.[10] The practice began in the fifteenth century when shogun Ashikaga Yoshimasa sent off a special piece of favorite pottery (a Chinese tea bowl) to China for repair. The bowl came back to him poorly repaired and quite ugly. The pieces were held together with crude metal staples. This offensive mess was unacceptable to the fussy shogun. He was furious. He sent it off again. This time it came back with a different kind of repair. Every crack on the vase was painted with gold, amplified, glorified with gold leaf.[11] The broken places were shown off; the very ruptures were highlighted, dramatized, made beautiful.

Shunryu Suzuki tells a story of Asahina Sogen, the enlightened abbot of the Rinzai temple at Engakuji, which reminds me of *kintsugi*. Many years after the abbot had attained enlightenment, he decided he wanted a wife. His followers were dismayed and shocked. He was such a perfect, pure master. How could he do this? He explained that "something was missing" and that he "wanted to be an ignorant, ordinary fellow after he attained enlightenment."[12] Suzuki said that Sogen wanted to "acknowledge his humanity. I think *that* is true enlightenment."[13] Sogen, it seems, wanted to affirm imperfection, explore his woundedness, cracks, and fissures—maybe even create a few. As if living with imperfections through revitalizing his Genjokoan was more real, more true, and certainly more human than anything else he could do.

As in the craft of *kintsugi*, we all must reckon with our woundedness and acknowledge our compulsive repetitions. We must welcome brokenness into our lives. Not only welcome it, but we must show it off—as if we are magnifying our custom-made Genjokoan for everyone to see.

### The Fracture

In any life there comes a time when tragedy occurs, one's own special vase slips and falls, the emotional tsunami strikes, one's inner world shatters, and nothing will ever be the same again. Whether we enter the world of the broken willingly, as did the abbot of Engakuji, or an unwelcome tragedy befalls us, the tsunami inevitably occurs. Knowing that our personal Genjokoan is embedded at the heart of our adversity, how can we come to embrace it, study it, and highlight it with gold?

As I explored the literature and attempted to formulate this notion of wounds leading to transformation, I began to encounter other writers, in addition to Leonard Cohen, who have attempted to tackle this same theme: Joan Didion, Joan Halifax, Christopher Hitchens, and Jeanette Winterson, to name a few.[14] I even found one writer who articulated this journey through the metaphor of *kintsugi*.

### BROKENNESS REVEALED

In his beautiful and poignant poem *Kintsugi*, Thomas Meyer both grieves and eulogizes the loss of his partner of almost forty years. Living with the pain—moment by moment, day by day—as he sits and writes beside his dying friend, he invites the reader to experience the gnawing cavernous hole in his gut so spacious that it created a "gap you could drive a Mack truck through." He describes "an emptiness that swept away the ground."[15] He is broken by the agony of his loss and the disorienting impact of his intense feelings during the long death watch—as his friend struggles in *articulo mortis*—in the grasp of death.[16]

In a similar vein, the Spanish poet and revolutionary hero Federico García Lorca writes about the importance of making one's pain manifest in its rawest form. He tells of duende, the dark muse, and its role in flamenco. Duende has a foundational role in helping the artist reveal the deep pain of the soul. This dark muse, perhaps best thought of as a possessive, demanding, and overpowering unconscious complex, must be fully experienced by the performer in order for its truth-bearing intensity to be expressed. Perhaps the most gripping form of duende in flamenco is found in the tragic *conte jondo,* or "deep singing." When caught up in the act of deep singing, the singer performs the soul's anguish. To do this authentically, the singer must *be the anguish.* According to Verbena Pastor, "unrequited passion, jealousy, despair, betrayal, awareness of death" are the subjects of flamenco.[17] It is not easy to be in this place of pain—nor to communicate it. Boaz Shalgi notes that "contained in such song is both the fear of expressing one's deepest pain and the urgent need to do exactly that."[18]

As the story goes, the great flamenco performer Pastora Pavon once sang beautifully, with all her exquisite technical skill, in a tavern in Cadiz, but the crowd was displeased. The listeners chided her for her "lack of duende." Something was missing. She was dumbstruck initially, but then she "stood up like a madwoman, aggrieved like a medieval mourner."[19] According to García Lorca's narrative, she then began to sing without voice:

> breathlessly . . . with a parched throat, but . . . with duende. She had succeeded in demolishing the entire structure of the song to make room for a duende furious and ablaze, friend of the silt laden winds.[20]

The impact was so powerful that the "listeners responded in a frenzy, tearing their shirts, like . . . believers crowding in religious furor . . . And how did she sing! Her voice . . . was a gush of blood ennobled by grief and truthfulness."[21]

We all yearn for this kind of truth in art and grace. And, when we hear it, when we see it, we cannot resist yelling out the name of God. Spanish audiences reward their performers in kind: "*Olé.*"[22]

### THE ROLE OF AUDIENCE AND COMMUNITY

How is it that flamenco audiences desire such intense displays of emotion? Do they identify with the performer or long for a deep catharsis of their own? Such a mutual, resonating catharsis seems to be at work in the presentation of Greek tragedies and other kinds of live theater. Catharsis seems to be most complete when it is mutually interactive. It is the shared experience that makes catharsis deeply fulfilling for both performer and audience. Both audience and performers long for involvement in what is emotionally true and emotionally real. As the psychoanalyst Jacques Lacan theorized, in the real we are longing for expression of those most deeply felt, raw emotional experiences that are beyond words and defy symbolic expression.[23] Despite this longing, the real is difficult for people to access. There is great fear of what is emotionally true. Most people spend their lives running from it. But there is a craving. "Something is missing" says the enlightened monk. "Something is missing" says everyman. It is essential that we go there.

Let us return to the Genjokoan for a moment, that ready-made problem that is our life work, be it a pernicious personality flaw, an addiction, a compulsion, a perversion, an intractable phobia. When we do work on it, it brings us to that place of emotional realness. Our effort takes us to the places of pain *and* to the places of emotional truth. Indeed, we like seeing others express what is emotionally true because the shared catharsis gives us courage and inspiration to embrace our own wounds and flaws.

So flamenco's deep singing is an act of *kintsugi,* and this is its appeal. The fractures and the excruciating pains are writ large and visible— for all to hear. The listeners know instinctively when the performer has gone beyond a mere technical display to the place of the real, to a place inspired by duende, to a place of deepest truth. Might we say that *this* is the emotional place where healing can begin? Getting to this place permits, even catalyzes, the transformation that people yearn for—as the deepest cracks and emotional wounds are revealed and shared.

## Wounded Healers

Arguably, the analyst plays a vital role in inviting emotional truth into the consulting room, having some of the characteristics of the flamenco audience. The analyst serves the function of the proverbial Socratic midwife, pulling and tugging, bringing forth the truth and invoking duende's visit, welcoming a song of blood. In this way the analyst is truly an active participant in an affectively packed drama unfolding in his or her presence. These dynamics are at the heart of Jung's notion of *participation mystique.* As Jung implied, we must become deeply involved with the patient's truth. The effective analyst must be open to the ever-present dynamics of projective identification, open to "feeling in our bones" what the patient is attempting to communicate to us beyond language or gesture. Open to the patient's inner world and responsive, even moved and changed by what occurs in the analysis, the analyst is a catalyst for pain as much as for change. We let their wounds affect us. We invite their wounds; we amplify them. And, of course, in this process it is inevitable that the patient will see our wounds as well as our mistakes. Through this dynamic, intersubjective process, both the analyst and the patient invariably change. Thinking of the psychoanalytic encounter this way makes the wounded healer a model of *kintsugi* within the therapeutic endeavor. Chiron, the mystical half man, half horse, the fisher king, and Prometheus—all wounded healers—symbolize every effective therapist, if not every man and woman.

## COMMUNITY

Community, in its diverse forms, provides the necessary alchemical vessel in which pain can first be acknowledged and expressed. Once received, it can then be contained, melted down, and eventually transformed through an ineffable process into something digestible and useable. Community can be the analytic couple, the family, the local setting, or the world. Transformation can occur at any and all levels of communal relatedness. From our personal conundrum to the *kintsugi*-like showing of the wounds to the flamenco song, we have witnessed the important role of community support and feedback. Might this be why communal rituals are so important to humankind and are found everywhere, in every culture and in all religions? We find them in synagogues, churches, mosques, sweat lodges, and the Sangha (the Buddhist term for spiritual community). The rituals of holy communion, seder, and Ramadan are among those that invite everyone—wounded healers, fractured saints, and broken sinners. Everyone is invited to the table.

In the psychoanalytic consulting room, the community is the therapeutic dyad, but healing communities occur naturally in many contexts. For example, in our local newspaper a man wrote the following after the tragic loss of his beloved teenage daughter:

> For when you give up trying to conceal your terrible wound, you find that others carry their own hidden scars. . . . [Their lives] are marked by their own personal losses, . . . their grief hidden just below the surface until it can be shared with another who understands.[24]

This letter expresses the meaning of exposing our wounds. "We are all more human than otherwise," said Harry Stack Sullivan. In light of Genjokoan and *kintsugi*, we might restate this to say, "We are all more *wounded* than otherwise." Through the acknowledgment of our wounds and the elaboration of our ready-made koans, a healing transformation is made possible and is emblazoned in gold.

## NOTES

1. Shinzen Young, *The Science of Enlightenment: Teaching and Meditation for Awakening Through Self-Investigation* (Boulder, CO: Sounds True, 1997), CD-ROM, Disc 5, Session 10.

2. Paul Russell, "The Role of Paradox in the Repetition Compulsion," in *Trauma, Repetition, and Affect Regulation: The Work of Paul Russell*, ed. Judith Guss Teicholz and Daniel Kriegman (New York: The Other Press, 1998), p. 2.

3. Shohaku Okumura, *Realizing Genjokoan: The Key to Dogen's Shobogenzo* (Boston: Wisdom Publications, 2010), p. 10.

4. Hakuun Yasutani, *Flowers Fall: Commentary on Zen Master Dogen's Genjokoan*, trans. Paul Jaffe (Boston: Shambhala, 1996), pp. 6–7.

5. *Ibid.*, p. 9.

6. Dairyu Michael Wenger, "Introduction: Three Commentaries on Dogen's Genjo Koan," in *Dogen's Genjo Koan: Three Commentaries*, ed. Mel Weitsman, Michael Wenger, and Shohaku Okumura, trans. Nishiari Bokusan, Shohaku Okumura, Shunryu Suzuki, Sojun Mel Weitsman, Kazuaki Tanahashi, and Dairyu Michael Wenger (Berkeley, CA: Counterpoint, 2011), p. 1.

7. *Ibid.*

8. Shunryu Suzuki, "Shunryu Suzuki Commentary on Genjo Koan," in Weitsman, Wenger, and Okumura, *Dogen's Genjo Koan*, p. 106.

9. *Ibid.*, p. 119.

10. Thomas Meyer, *Kintsugi* (Chicago: Flood Editions, 2011), p. 1.

11. Blake Gopnik, "'Golden Seams: The Japanese Art of Mending Ceramics' at Freer," *The Washington Post*, March 2, 2009, accessed September 30, 2012, at http://www.washingtonpost.com/wp-dyn/content/article/2009/03/02/AR 2009030202723.html.

12. Suzuki, "Commentary on Genjo Koan," p. 118.

13. *Ibid.*

14. Joan Didion, *The Year of Magical Thinking* (New York: Vintage Books, 2006); Joan Halifax, *The Fruitful Darkness: A Journey though Buddhist Practice and Tribal Wisdom* (New York: Grove Press, 1993); Christopher Hitchens, *Mortality* (New York: Twelve, 2012); Jeanette Winterson, *Why Be Happy When You Could Be Normal?* (New York: Grove Press, 2011).

15. Meyer, *Kintsugi*, pp. 11, 15.

16. *Ibid.*, p. x.

17. Verbena Pastor, "The Dark Side of Creativity: The Function of Duende and God Battler in the Writings of García Lorca and Kazantzakis," in *Creativity, Spirituality, and Transcendence: Paths to Integrity and Wisdom in the Mature Self*, ed. Melvin E. Miller and Susanne R. Cook-Greuter (Stamford, CT: Ablex Publishing Corporation, 2000), p. 27.

18. Boaz Shalgi, "*Por el Flamenco*: The Roots of Pain, The Roots of Life," (paper presented at the International Association for Relational Psychoanalysis and Psychotherapy, March 4, 2012).

19. Pastor, "The Dark Side of Creativity," p. 39.

20. F. García Lorca, *Obras Completas* [*Complete Works*] (Madrid: Aguilar, 1960), p. 40.

21. *Ibid.*

22. Pastor, "The Dark Side of Creativity," p. 26.

23. Darian Leader and Judy Groves, *Introducing Lacan* (London: Icon Books, 1995), p. 61.

24. "On Grieving, Healing, and Community," *The Bridge*, March 1–14, 2012, p. 14.

# HAIKU AND THE HEALING WAY

## DAVID H. ROSEN

B uddhism and Taoism have been a central part of my work in depth psychology. For example, I explore in print the therapeutic value of egolessness, the main principle of Buddhism, in *The Healing Spirit of Haiku*.[1] Through haiku, one has access to the individual and collective unconscious in a way similar to the Jungian practice of active imagination. Another example is my depth psychological approach to helping suicidally depressed patients through egocide (symbolic death of the self-destructive ego or shadow) and transformation to one's authentic self.[2] Both painting and haiku have been an integral part of my own individuation process. *Haibun*, which combines haiku and narrative, is the genre of my forthcoming autobiography, *Lost in Aotearoa: Finding My Way Home*. *Haibun* represents a journey; in the case of memoir it traces a lifelong pilgrimage to one's true self and realization of no-self. Being a foolish being, I am drawn to Buddhism and in particular Shin Buddhism and its focus on Other power, which is similar to Jung's depth psychology.[3] The spiritual

David H. Rosen, M.D., was the initial holder of the McMillan Professorship in Analytical Psychology at Texas A&M University. He continues to host the Fay Lectures and edit the Fay Books in Analytical Psychology series. He currently lives in Eugene, Oregon, and is affiliate professor in psychiatry at the Oregon Health and Science University. He is the author of more than a hundred articles, many poems, and ten books. His most recent work is a chapbook "Clouds and More Clouds" and his memoir, *Lost in Aotearoa: Finding My Way Home* (forthcoming).

goal of *haibun* is to glean the essence of one's life's journey and the practical goal is to describe meaningful experiences, the more personal the better, because then they are the most archetypal or universal.

### PERSONAL JOURNEY

Dr. Nada is my name—
my card
nothing on it

My own journey toward self-realization and egocide began in 1963 when I registered with the Selective Service Board at the age of eighteen. Being a conscientious objector to war, I had to write an essay justifying my position which helped me to realize at the dawn of my adulthood that war made no sense and was ethically wrong. In fact, I used this quote by John F. Kennedy as an epigraph at the beginning of my essay: "War will exist until that distant day when the conscientious objector enjoys the same reputation and prestige that the warrior does today."[4]

Seven years later, during my internship as a physician, I was drafted; however, I was granted conscientious objector status and ordered to do alternative service for two years in a California state mental institution. This experience opened an old wound related to my father being shell-shocked as a navy physician in the Pacific theater during World War II. In a period of profound depression that occurred during my psychiatric residency, I sought help from a Freudian analyst. Then as a result of readings in seminars about Jung's psychology and research on people who had jumped off the Golden Gate Bridge and survived, I began to see a Jungian analyst. It was during this period that I coined the term *egocide* and realized that the death of the ego (or suicidal self) is a meaningful alternative to suicide. I got the idea for this from one of the survivors, who said, "Dr. Rosen, the identity that drove me to the Golden Gate Bridge, parked my car, wrote a suicide note, walked out to the first suspension tower, and leapt *died*." I knew that the label "failed suicide" made no sense, and I understood that the ego identity (the suicidal self) that had precipitated the leap off the bridge had been killed, like the serpent that sheds its skin. The most amazing thing to witness was the experience of transformation of despair to hope that followed.

Buddhism—
no ego or self
to kill

Subsequently, I joined the San Francisco C. G. Jung Institute and eventually became an analyst. During my long career as professor of analytical psychology and psychiatry at Texas A&M University, my research team's motto was "Research is me-search." My interest in healing, Jung's spiritual psychology, Buddhism, Taoism, and the healing spirit of haiku all relate to egocide, finding inner peace, and allowing it to evolve over the years.

### INNER PEACE

What facilitates inner peace? Activities that allow space for the emergence of egolessness: meditation, prayer, and being in and with nature, as well as active imagination and creativity.[5] Over the past three decades I have pursued research involving egocide, transforming depression, and healing the soul through creativity. My research team has found that artistic practices like drawing mandalas, writing haiku poetry, and ikebana are healing and related to improving mental health.[6] Furthermore, in medical students with the s/s genotype of the serotonin transporter gene (5-HTT PR), who are most vulnerable to stress-linked depression, we have found that hope and spiritual meaning buffer or moderate the expression of depressive symptoms.[7]

At the age of sixty-five, a book entitled *Do Nothing: Inner Peace for Everyday Living*, drew me like iron to a magnet.[8] I found affirmation for "listening to life," enjoying the silences, staying in moments of sorrow, happiness, pain, and joy, not analyzing (hard for an analyst) or judging, but allowing "the soul to find its own destiny."[9] As Paul Tillich maintained, the key is to have the courage "to be" in the face of nothingness.[10] Nishitani Keiji focused on the same idea in *Religion and Nothingness*: being is about letting go and is born of non-being.[11] In a similar vein, Taoism upholds *wu-wei*, or effortless action and the virtue of doing by not doing.[12]

## FUTILITY OF EFFORT

No
mind—
cleaning the birdbath

Buddhist monk and founder of Shin Buddhism, Shinran, makes
the distinction between self power and Other power. I find this useful
in shedding light on egocide and my own spiritual journey. Shinran
maintains that religious insight lies within the discovery that our own
efforts are futile; we cannot rise above the foolishness that is inherent
in human nature. Ultimately, whether one is good or evil, accomplished
or mediocre, young or old, makes no difference because all human
beings are foolishly ego-centered and utterly incapable of producing
the turnaround to non-ego, or Other power, through their own efforts.
Therefore, religious consciousness demands that one penetrate the
reality of one's foolishness.[13] Only by taking refuge in that which
transcends the ego, namely Amida Buddha or Other power, can one
eventually realize enlightenment, or what Jung termed *individuation*.
The loss of faith in our own capacities opens up the way to the absolute
that is within us at each moment.[14]

Amongst the stones
no more
loneliness

For me and my patients, creativity has been a way of accessing that
which is beyond self power. Throughout my career and in my personal
life, I have found that egocide opens the door to healing. The false self
that was hell-bent on self-destructive behavior dies and the true self is
reborn.[15] The death of my suicidal self enabled me to join art and science
in my personal and professional life. More recently, as I reflected upon
my life story in the process of writing my memoir, the power of that
which is beyond ego became real. I realized that the story often wrote
me instead of the other way around.

## LOVE FINDS US

Inner peace and the surrender of the self is also related to love and
synchronicity; "when we do not look for love, love finds us."[16] In 2005,
I went to the South Island of New Zealand on a sabbatical to become

lost in order to find myself. I tend to meditate while I walk, becoming a part of nature for a moment. Haiku poetry is the product of this creative process of active imagination. After being there for a month, walking daily by the shore at Governors Bay, I met a woman named Lanara. I sat down next to her on a bench at Allendale and offered her half of an apple, which she took. She had walked from the jetty at Governors Bay and, since I was going there, we walked together. My first question was typically American, "What do you do?" She answered, "Nothing. I'm not into doing, just being." That Buddhist-like response silenced me, and we both walked quietly, observing nature in all its beauty.

> What joy
> finding you here in winter—
> small purple flower

Lanara is now my wife, and we view our meeting and being together as synchronicity and divine love.

Although not Buddhist or Taoist, I feel a kinship to these spiritual philosophies. Affirming my path to the sacred goes back to many deep and meaningful conversations with like-minded colleagues. My personal and professional interest in the death of the self and the healing value of creativity are inspired by Buddhist and Taoist principles of egolessness. Ultimately, my own path toward self-surrender gains expression through the spiritual practices of haiku and *haibun* which join an appreciation of nature with a creative power beyond the ego.

> My life—
> a long
> slow rain

## NOTES

1. David H. Rosen and Joel Weishaus, *The Healing Spirit of Haiku* (Berkeley, CA: North Atlantic Books, 2004).

2. David H. Rosen, *Transforming Depression: Healing the Soul through Creativity*, 3rd ed. (York Beach, ME: Nicolas-Hays, 2002).

3. Taitetsu Unno, *River of Fire, River of Water: An Introduction to the Pure Land Tradition of Shin Buddhism* (New York: Doubleday, 1998).

4. John F. Kennedy, JFK Library and Museum, accessed July 7, 2010, at http://www.jfklibrary.org/Historical+Resources/Archives/Reference+Desk/Quotations+of+John+F+Kennedy.htm.

5. See Thich Nhat Hanh, *Peace Is Every Step* (New York: Bantum Books, 1991); Thich Nhat Hanh, *Touching Peace* (Berkeley, CA: Parallex Press, 1992); Maggie Oman, ed., *Prayers for Healing* (Berkeley, CA: Conari Press, 1997); Henry David Thoreau, *Walden: A Life in the Woods* (New York: Houghton Mifflin, 2004); C. G. Jung, *Jung on Active Imagination*, ed. Joan Chodorow (Princeton, NJ: Princeton University Press, 1997); John Daido Loori, *The Zen of Creativity: Cultivating Your Artistic Life* (New York: Ballatine Books, 2004).

6. Patti Henderson, David H. Rosen, and Nathan Mascaro, "Empirical Study on the Healing Nature of Mandalas," *Psychology of Aesthetics, Creativity, and the Arts* 1(3, 2007): 148–154; Rosen and Weishaus, *The Healing Spirit of Haiku*; Kittredge Stephenson, "The Healing Nature of Haiku: An Empirical Study" (master of science thesis, Texas A&M University, 2009); Milena D. Sotirova-Kohli, "Archetypal Creativity and Healing: An Empirical Study of Floral Design (Ikebana)" (master of science thesis, Texas A&M University, 2009).

7. David H. Rosen, et al., "Depression in Medical Students: Gene-Environment Interactions," *Annals of Behavioral Science and Medical Education* 16(2, 2010): 8–14.

8. Siroj Sorajjakool, *Do Nothing: Inner Peace for Everyday Living* (West Conshohocken, PA: Templeton Foundation Press, 2009).

9. *Ibid.*, pp. 46, 123.

10. Paul Tillich, *The Courage to Be* (New Haven, CT: Yale University Press, 1952).

11. Keiji Nishitani, *Religion and Nothingness* (Berkeley, CA: University of California Press, 1983).

12. Lao Tzu, *Tao Te Ching: The Classic Book of Integrity and the Way*, trans. Victor A. Mair (New York: Bantam Books, 1990).

13. Elizabeth McManaman Grosz, "Reading Nishida through Shinran: Absolute Nothingness, Other Power, and Religious Consciousness," *Journal of Buddhist Philosophy* (forthcoming).

14. *Ibid.*, p. 7.

15. See D. W. Winnicott, "Fear of Breakdown," in *The British School of Psychoanalysis: The Independent Tradition*, ed. Gregorio Kohon (New Haven, CT: Yale University Press, 1986), pp. 173–182.

16. Sorajjakool, *Do Nothing*, p. 126.

# BUDDHISM, PSYCHOANALYSIS, AND THE CARE OF HOMELESS PEOPLE

DEBORAH ANNA LUEPNITZ

I felt it shelter to speak to you.
                    —Emily Dickinson, Letter #533

The Buddha not only taught compassion for all beings, including the suffering poor, he also urged all who seek enlightenment to move *from home to homelessness*. Forgoing material possessions and domesticity can help clarify the Dharma. To this day, monks and nuns choose a celibate life, owning nothing but their robes and rice bowls. There are also Buddhist teachers—for example, Tetsugen Bernard Glassman, in the United States—who conduct "street retreats" during which they live for weeks at a time among homeless people.[1] In a recent interview about homelessness as a social problem, the Dalai Lama remarked: "On some level, I am also homeless. Being homeless is sometimes useful, because you realize that in many places you can

Deborah Anna Luepnitz, Ph.D., is a psychoanalyst practicing in Philadelphia. She is on the clinical faculty of the Department of Psychiatry at the University of Pennsylvania School of Medicine and on the faculty of the Institute for Relational Psychoanalysis of Philadelphia. She is the author of *Schopenhauer's Porcupines: Intimacy and Its Dilemmas* and was a contributing author to *The Cambridge Companion to Lacan*. Luepnitz is the founder of Insight for All (IFA), a pro bono psychotherapy project for homeless adults and families.

find a new home." But His Holiness was quick to acknowledge the profound distress of the very poor. "For people without a home, it is almost like they have no basis from which to conduct their lives. They have no anchor. That is very sad."[2]

Ultimately, the Buddhist ideal of homelessness does not point as much to a renunciation of shelter as it does to finding a spiritual home within. It refers to following a Middle Way between the extremes of hedonism and asceticism and attending to the basic needs of one's fellow beings.

The major cause of homelessness in the United States is the lack of affordable housing. What we as a nation could do to reduce suffering would be to restore housing subsidies to previous levels and add services for those who struggle with addictions or schizophrenia.[3] The focus of this chapter, however, is not social policy but the potential contributions of Buddhism and psychoanalysis to those who are already homeless.

The Buddhist notion of *dependent origination*—a fundamental albeit somewhat elusive concept—points to the interrelatedness of all beings. Put simply, it means that the sharp divisions we perceive between self and other, person and environment, are convenient illusions. Keeping dependent origination in mind means realizing that we who live indoors are connected to those who do not. Indeed, recent events have reminded people that most of us are but one hurricane or medical catastrophe away from destitution.

Some may wonder what psychoanalysis has to offer on the subject of homelessness, given its reputation as elitist. While it's true that Freud emphasized the role of the fee in helping patients feel invested in the treatment, he changed his mind about this—something too few analysts seem to realize.[4] In a beautiful speech given in Budapest in 1918, Freud predicted that "the conscience of society will awake" and that rich and poor alike would have access to analytic treatment.[5] This was not simply wishful thinking. Over the decade that followed, ten free clinics sprang up in seven European countries, treating farmers, factory workers, chambermaids, and the unemployed. Elizabeth Danto recovers this history in *Freud's Free Clinics: Psychoanalysis and Social Justice, 1918–1938*.[6] After the Nazi takeover of those clinics, free psychoanalysis on a large scale disappeared, with only pockets of pro bono work remaining in various countries, including the United States and Great Britain.[7]

In Philadelphia, in 2005, I started IFA (Insight for All), a small program which connects psychoanalysts willing to work for free with homeless people who have chosen to leave the street and reside at Philadelphia's Project HOME. Founded in 1989 by Sister of Mercy Mary Scullion and her friend Joan Dawson McConnen, Project HOME has helped more than 8,000 people break the cycle of poverty, addiction, and homelessness. Residents are not simply sheltered; they are offered medical care, job training, and opportunities for political engagement. IFA offers some of them psychoanalysis as well.

Psychoanalytic theory reminds us that the first home we inhabit is the mother's body. At birth, we enter the more open housing of her arms and the arms of fathers and other caregivers. If all goes reasonably well, the baby learns what it means to feel warm, safe, contained. When caregivers respond lovingly, the child learns that its needs are bearable and have meaning. But if trauma occurs—physical violence, sexual assault, neglect, or abandonment—the foundation for a true self is not formed. One consequence can be an inability to be housed anywhere. I once believed that only a heartless person could say, "Some homeless people don't even want help," but the fact is that many for whom the experience of family and home has been ruinous will always chafe at containment. What is missing for such individuals is the sense of an internal home—a feeling of being "well in one's own skin" that makes it possible to recognize a physical abode as habitable and an emotional connection as benign.

In the example below, I will describe the treatment of a woman who had lived for four years on the street before coming indoors. I held our sessions at her residence—something most IFA analysts do—as we have found that asking patients to come to us ruptures the protective skin offered by Project HOME.

CLINICAL FRAGMENT

"Lenore" was a sixty-three-year-old mixed-race woman who had lived with her mother and stepfather most of her life. They died within months of each other, and Lenore was completely at a loss. She ended up on a neighbor's couch, then in a shelter, and finally on the street. For several years, she politely declined outreach services, walking many miles per day ("for something to do"), panhandling, and sleeping in the rat-infested subway concourse by night. One evening she agreed to try Project HOME and seemed to appreciate the plentiful food and warm, clean dormitory. Staff members liked her sweet smile but were concerned about the full-body rash she had arrived with—something she would not discuss. In the six months since she arrived, she hadn't bathed or changed clothes. She would sit on a sofa near the door all day, every day, staring ahead, not even glancing at television. The scant information we had about her included a diagnosis of schizophrenia and a history of learning disabilities. Now she was afraid to leave the building, and staff asked if she would like to speak with a psychotherapist.

In our first session Lenore said: "I'm afraid. I'd like to go out and get fresh air, but I just can't." She couldn't tell me what she was afraid of. "Just afraid," she repeated. I asked about her experiences on the street, but she was not forthcoming. "I managed" was her typical reply. I wanted to get a sense of her life before she became homeless, but again, it seemed hard for her to discuss the past. She did disclose that she had married at age eighteen, stayed married for five years, and bore two children now in their thirties, with whom she had long ago lost contact.

Two months into our work, Lenore opened a session asking: "Deborah, could you spare $1.49?" I smiled and said, "That's a very specific amount!" She said she wanted to buy some Tastykakes. She had only a few teeth left, and this was the only dessert she enjoyed. I was a bit flummoxed. I happened to know that she had just received her first disability check and could have easily afforded to buy sweets. She was painfully thin, however, and although psychoanalysis is a talking cure—not a financial one—I was aware of how much I wanted to feed her. She disarmed me completely by taking the analytic stance of asking me to "just think about it."

During the course of the next week, I thought of little else. I thought of the psychoanalysts—above all, Donald Winnicott—who might bring her this simple treat in order to foster therapeutic connection. Winnicott initiated a trend that has been referred to as the maternalization of the analyst. He believed that by taking the role of good-enough mother, he could help repair the damage done to the patient in childhood.[8] I could almost see him pulling a pack of Tastykakes out of his vest pocket and watching the glow in her eyes.

However, another important influence on my thinking has been the French psychoanalyst, Jacques Lacan, who did not see the therapist's role as maternal.[9] Lacan argued against the analyst's gratification of the patient's demands since it's often just a way of making ourselves feel better. Rather than succumb to the rescue impulse, he favored a committed listening for (unconscious) desire.[10]

In the session that followed, Lenore made a slightly different request: "Could you bring me something you've baked?" Now we had a new area to explore. She told me a bit about things she had made with her grandmother as a child, and she had a lot of questions about my own skills in the kitchen. She imagined me as a talented chef and was surprised to hear me say, "I'm actually not the greatest cook." She spoke more freely in that session than in the earlier ones, and I ended up telling her that therapists bring food for thought, not cake or money. I asked how she felt about this, and she replied, "A little disappointed, I guess, but I understand." I asked if there were some other way she might get the snack cakes, and she said, "I'm not sure. Maybe I can."

That week when Kitty, Project HOME's cook, asked which women would like to go in the van with her to the grocery store, Lenore—to everyone's surprise—volunteered. This would be her first time outdoors in six months, and apparently she ambled through the aisles buying several soft desserts. On her return, she washed up a bit and put on a clean shirt. Lenore was thrilled to tell me her good news and sat eating a whole package of snack cakes, licking her fingers.

We talked about the fact that my saying no to her request for money or cake had made it necessary for her to be more independent. She still wouldn't go out alone, however, even to walk a block away. I began to think of her agoraphobia in terms of Winnicott's essay, "Fear of Breakdown."[11] There he describes people who live for decades with a sense that they are going to fall apart and who must ward this off by compulsive behaviors or avoidance of places or relationships. Winnicott found with many such patients evidence that there had actually been a breakdown—in infancy, childhood, or young adulthood. If a breakdown occurs but isn't experienced due to dissociation, then there is no way of grieving the experience—and no sense of an ending. I believe there is a lot to this idea that what one fears most has already happened. I eventually suggested to Lenore that the thing she feared—something bad happening if she "left home"—had already happened.

She simply had been too busy surviving to realize it. She seemed puzzled but agreed to think about it.

In one of our next sessions, Lenore told me that she had been on an airplane once in her life—on a trip to Florida with a friend. She couldn't tell me when except to say: "It was when the Challenger rocket blew up with that teacher on it! The teacher died; it was so sad!" She helped me understand that she associated leaving home with that trip and the trip with catastrophic loss. Her emphasizing the teacher's death made me wonder if it resonated with an early loss in her life—possibly of her biological father—or even a part of herself. Might it also refer to me, given that I had been her most recent "challenger"?

What happened around this time in our work together was that Lenore became acutely interested in my physical needs. I was not allowed to leave a session without buttoning my coat and tying my scarf. "It's cold out there!" One snowy day, she worried that my car wouldn't start. Without thinking, I said, "Don't worry—I always walk here." She was aghast. "Why do you walk? What's wrong with your car? DON'T YOU HAVE A CAR?" I always thanked her for her concern and was struck by how awkward those interactions were. I also couldn't help noticing that while scrutinizing my self-care, she would become more organized and articulate. I, in contrast, began to stammer. I couldn't seem to find the words to tell her I was all right. "It's not that cold. I like to walk; it's healthy . . ." Nothing I said made her nod in recognition. I felt a little crazy trying to defend my utterly reasonable lifestyle to a homeless woman who remained visibly upset by what she perceived to be my lack of access to goods and services.

There is nothing unusual about having a countertransference response like this with any patient. What was peculiar was how long the dynamic continued—how long I felt weirdly, inexplicably ashamed. Although I was never able to deliver this as an interpretation, I believe that what she was saying was: "Imagine a woman walking alone for long distances in the cold!" She was not able to cry with me about her own homeless years of pain and humiliation, battling the elements. Instead, she seemed to experience them vicariously through me. We had reversed roles. I was the struggling person, defending my right to do things my way, asking not to be judged too harshly, and she was the voice of society, of the stern parent, the censorious other.

In Buddhist terms, we might say this small and temporary exchange of subjectivities is nothing surprising. When we contemplate dependent origination we are reminded of the oneness of all minds. As a clinician, the psychoanalytic formulation that is most helpful, however, is known as projective identification. It is a defense mechanism in which affects that are too painful to contain are split off and projected onto another person. Instead of expressing or even experiencing her own shame, she had stored it in me and could observe it from a distance. We can say that at an unconscious level, she needed me to know something of what she herself had to feel all the time. Benedetti summarized the analyst's task well:

> The psychotherapy of psychosis is only analytical insofar as we are prepared to analyze ourselves continually in the encounter with the patient, to ask ourselves at each instant what is the significance of our words, and what are the links we propose as regards the patient's identity.[12]

An important turn of events began with Lenore telling me that another Project HOME resident was moving into her own apartment. I asked if she would miss this young woman, and Lenore said: "A little. She was the same age as my daughter." She had always refused to talk about her children. I asked if it would be all right to explore this topic, and she said, "Maybe next week." Staff called me a few days later to say that Lenore had begun hearing voices and asked to be hospitalized. For the following three weeks, we held sessions on the ward. Lenore told me only then that she had taken an overdose when her daughter was born and that the infant had been taken away and raised by her grandmother. I had never seen her express sadness and shame before. Those weeks seemed to do her good, as she allowed a physician to treat her rash and stomach ulcer. She also agreed to bathe and wash her hair for the first time. All of this led to her sleeping and eating better than she had in years.

Our work was just beginning to deepen when, seven months in, she announced the desire to contact a half sister she hadn't seen in a decade. Lenore's half sister immediately invited her to live with her in a state several hundred miles away. It took only weeks to make the move. Lenore was particularly excited to learn that her half sister's daughter was about to give birth to twins.

Although our work was cut short, we both felt it had been valuable. On several occasions, she said: "I've felt better ever since you wanted to talk to me." Therapy gave her the impetus to leave the building for the first time and begin to care for herself. Mention of her daughter had brought on the crisis that led to her hospitalization where she felt safe enough to at least begin to talk about the breakdown she had experienced as a new mother. Feeling rested once her ulcer was treated, she felt bold enough to contact her relative (of whom we had known nothing) despite their having fallen out long ago. Perhaps she felt she could repair the time of her own early motherhood with these soon-to-be-born babies, for whom she would not be responsible.

Lenore let me know she wasn't interested in more therapy at the moment. I knew of no one who worked pro bono in her new town, but I gave her half sister the name of a community mental health center and offered to consult with any future therapists.

Although our work together might be deemed a modest success, I was bereft at how much remained undone.

What's a psychoanalyst to do with the worry that things will fall apart? Some therapists send cards in the mail, often with offers of prayer. There is nothing wrong with this, but I have found that the most helpful thing in such situations is a Buddhist meditation practice called *tonglen*. When we practice *tonglen*, we breathe in the suffering of the other, breathing out to them our health and well-being. I breathe in Lenore's fear, shame, fragility. I breathe out my own hope, equanimity, strength. A question that inevitably arises is whether or not this taking in of the other's suffering can do damage. At a lecture at the Shambhala Center of Philadelphia in 2007, Traleg Rinpoche explained that if we breathe in the suffering of a person with cancer, for example, we're not at risk for getting that person's cancer! What we take in is the suffering, which is non-material and is burned off by our *bodhicitta*. Bodhicitta—a term that combines the Sanskrit words for wisdom and compassion—refers to the enlightened mind's intention to reduce the suffering of all sentient beings.

Both the *tonglen* meditation and the analytic practice of attunement to countertransference can be understood as skillful ways of responding to dependent origination. Attending to countertransference is a receptive practice; it allows us to understand that what arises in us may originate in the other's suffering. *Tonglen* is an active means for working with that very suffering.

I find *tonglen* a particularly meaningful practice on behalf of homeless patients who have endured so much in a world that would rather cast them out than keep them in mind and heart. *Tonglen* is a way of staying connected or—more accurately—of honoring the connection that exists among us.

## NOTES

1. Christopher Queen, "Buddhism, Activism, and Unknowing: A Day with Bernard Glassman," *Tikkun* 13, no. 1 (1998): 64–66.

2. Danielle Batist, "Exclusive Interview with Dalai Lama: 'Homeless Should Not Feel Desperate,'" *One Step Away*, July 2012, p. 9.

3. Dennis Culhane and Steven Metraux, "Rearranging the Deck Chairs or Reallocating the Lifeboats?" *Journal of the American Planning Association* 74, no. 1 (2008): 111–121.

4. Sigmund Freud, "On Beginning the Treatment" (1913), in *The Standard Edition of the Complete Works of Sigmund Freud*, vol. 12 (London: Hogarth Press, 1991), pp. 123–144.

5. Sigmund Freud, "Lines of Advance in Psychoanalytic Psychotherapy," in *The Standard Edition of the Complete Works of Sigmund Freud*, vol. 17 (London: Hogarth Press, 1991), p. 166.

6. Elizabeth Danto, *Freud's Free Clinics: Psychoanalysis and Social Justice 1918–1938* (New York: Columbia University Press, 2005).

7. See Neil Altman, *The Analyst in the Inner City* (Hillsdale, NJ: Analytic Press, 1995); and June Campbell, "Homelessness and Containment: A Psychotherapy Project with Homeless People and Workers in the Homeless Field," *Psychoanalytic Psychotherapy* 10, no. 3 (2006): 157–174.

8. Donald W. Winnicott, *Playing and Reality* (London: Tavistock, 1971).

9. Deborah Luepnitz, *Schopenhauer's Porcupines* (New York: Basic Books, 2002); and "Thinking in the Space between Winnicott and Lacan," *International Journal of Psychoanalysis* 90, no. 5 (2009): 957–981.

10. Jacques Lacan, *Écrits: A Selection*, trans. Alan Sheridan (New York: Norton, 1977).

11. Donald W. Winnicott, "Fear of Breakdown," in *Psychoanalytic Explorations*, ed. Clare Winnicott, Ray Shepherd, and Madeline Davis (Cambridge, MA: Harvard University Press, 1989), pp. 87–95.

12. Gaetano Benedetti, *La mort dans l'âme. Psychothérapie de la schizophrénie: existence et transfert* [*Death in the Soul. The Psychotherapy of Schizophrenia: Transference and Existence*], trans. P. Faugeras and D. Faugeras (Ramonville, Sainte-Anne: Érès, 1995), p. 25.

# LAGNIAPPE

# Buddhism—A Personal Experience

## Leslie de Galbert

My relationship with—I might even say my love for—Buddhism could be called pedestrian and has come to me rather late in life, in a manner always highly prized by Jung: that of experience. I mean nothing pejorative by *pedestrian*, rather I relate to its etymology, and in using this word I think of my walk through life. A further association comes in recalling that I experienced my first close contact with Buddhist culture during three weeks as a pedestrian, trekking high in the Himalayan mountains in November 1999, from the tiny village of Lukla to the base camp of Mount Everest. It is difficult to describe the prevailing ambience in a such a geographical setting, void—at the time—of any motor vehicle and having very little communication

Leslie de Galbert, B.A., D.E.S.S. (Diplôme d'Études Supérieures Spécialisées), D.U. (Diplôme Universitaire) was born and raised in New Orleans and moved to France after earning her undergraduate degree in philosophy at Hollins University in Virginia. She completed her graduate studies in clinical psychology at the Université de Paris VII and earned a postgraduate degree in psycho-oncology at the medical school of the Université de Paris VI. She trained as a Jungian analyst at the Société Française de Psychologie Analytique and is a member of the International Society of Analytical Psychology. She has taught in the training program of the S.F.P.A. and is currently supervising analysts in training in Tbilisi, Republic of Georgia, under the auspices of the I.A.A.P. She has published articles in the *Cahiers jungiens de psychanalyse* and lectured on Jung's *Red Book* in France and in Belgium. She maintains a private practice in Paris.

with the outside world; one where the inhabitants live so close to the earth, in harsh material circumstances and what I felt to be in communion with the Buddhist monasteries sprinkled among and between the villages. The absence of our usual Western modes of living, for example, of motor vehicles, machines, telephones, and such, did not evoke the sense of something missing or any kind of lack or emptiness. Today I might say that any lack or emptiness there might have been could rather be that which Buddhists strive toward through the practice of their philosophy, what we might call the experience of oneness with the no-thingness of the world. My experience was one of sensing a people whose human suffering, material and existential, was characterized, and even mitigated, by its being enveloped or rooted in Buddhist culture and philosophy. There was a palpable feeling of what today we very commonly call mindfulness. I later felt the same ambience in my much less close contact with the people of Bhutan during a visit there and with the Burmese in the villages on the waters around Lake Inle in Myanmar.

Until these travels, my knowledge of Buddhism and other Eastern contemplative practices or religions had been almost purely intellectual. As an undergraduate philosophy major in college, I had taken a few courses in Eastern philosophy and religion. Through my training as a Jungian psychoanalyst, I came to know more deeply—yet still rather intellectually—the meaning of mandalas and the collective nature of what they symbolize relative to our human psyche, conscious and unconscious.

Then, about five years ago, I began the practice of yoga with a woman deeply engaged in a holistic approach to yoga and who had traveled to India many times, including to Dharamsala. Although I had done yoga before, it was different this time, and I imagine that this difference was related to my travels and to this new teacher. Yoga seemed, this time around, to incarnate what I knew about Buddhism and, more important, what I had begun to feel during my travels in Buddhist countries with regard to a living and lived philosophy.

There is a final ingredient that made possible the singular privilege I had of being able to present Jung's *Red Book* as a gift to

His Holiness the Dalai Lama in Dharamsala in October 2011. Thanks to an important friendship, I was invited to attend a Mind and Life Institute's conference, (Ecology, Ethics, and Interdependence), and thus to this gift-giving experience. While in graduate school in clinical psychology in France in the late 1980s, I became close friends with probably the only other American in the graduate department, and she at that time met her future husband who—perhaps unbeknownst even to him—was in the process of creating what was to become the Mind and Life Institute.[1] Cocreated by Francisco Varela and Adam Engle, with the participation and full support of His Holiness, the Mind and Life Institute's history is well documented on its website. Through Amy Cohen, Francisco's wife and my friend, I remained vaguely aware over the years of this remarkable organization's existence and activities. It was only recently, however, that I reconnected with what Amy had experienced during all of the intervening years at the heart of the organization. When she invited me to a Mind and Life conference in Delhi in 2010, I accepted with enthusiasm, and with even more enthusiasm the following year when I was invited to the more intimate meeting to be held in the private residence of His Holiness in Dharamsala.[2] The Dalai Lama has a deep and abiding belief that science, and in particular the neurosciences, are an essential and fundamental vehicle for furthering our striving to reduce the suffering of humans and promote chances for more peace and compassion in the world. He is unequivocally committed to supporting the Mind and Life Institute and participates actively in the conferences and symposia that the institute organizes. In so doing, he affirms the bridge that he has helped to build between the contemplative sciences such as Buddhism, on the one hand, and modern Western science on the other.

It seemed to me that Jung had also perceived this connection between East and West, between Buddhism, which he first came to know through Richard Wilhelm, and the understanding of the human psyche that he had approached first through the Western science of psychiatry and then through his analytical psychology. I thought of Jung as almost a precursor of those who conceived and founded the Mind and Life Institute. Thus my desire to bring Jung's

*Red Book* as a gift to His Holiness. The experience of carrying *The Red Book* all the way to Dharamsala—not an easy place to reach!—was surpassed only by the intense emotion of presenting the book to His Holiness and conversing for a few minutes with him on the subject of Jung and *The Red Book*. As he turned pages, looking with interest at the brilliantly colored images while we spoke, he remarked on their beauty and told me that he knew of Jung. My lasting hope is that despite the unrelenting pace his obligations impose upon him, he will be able to find a bit of time to explore this work of Jung's. I gave His Holiness a letter to explain the meaning of the gift:

October 2011

Your Holiness,

It is an honor for me to participate in this meeting of Mind and Life in Dharamsala, thanks to my dear friend Amy Cohen Varela, as it is also an honor for me to be involved with the Summer Research Institute in memory of Francisco.

Please forgive me if you already know this Red Book created by the Swiss psychiatrist Carl Gustav Jung (1875–1961) and allow me to explain in a few words why we have brought it here as a gift to you. In a word, I believe that the book itself may be seen as an impressive example of one of Mind and Life's primary goals: discerning and exploring the connections between Western science and contemplative, Eastern traditions. This, of course, was *not* Jung's goal in creating the book, but I believe that this is what the Red Book became as Jung followed the path that his unconscious set him out upon: the book became an illustration of how the East and the West are connected at the heart and core of the human psyche.

Carl Jung was a visionary in every sense of the word, but he was first and foremost a psychiatrist whose scientific side (as a medical doctor) was rooted in his lifelong interest and study of philosophy and whose personal life began as the son and grandson of Protestant pastors. All his life he was troubled by religious and philosophical questions. He became a medical doctor, specialized in psychiatry and began his career working with psychotic patients, mostly schizophrenic. He sought understanding of the *contents* of their delusions, and tried to find *meaning* in what his patients manifested in their hallucinations. In the end, he believed that these contents have symbolic value.

Jung came to know Sigmund Freud (1856–1939) in 1900 and they became intimate colleagues in 1906, but differences brewed and they separated in a quite violent manner in 1913. Jung was devastated and he entered a period of his life that would last for several years. He claimed to have "lost his soul" and set out on an inward journey to "re-find" it, and to find a path possible for him without the scientific and personal relationship with Freud.

In 1913–1914, Jung noted his "visionary experiences" in which he "saw" and "listened to" imagined figures, and then for one year, he wrote out stories using the "visions" to dialogue with the figures, and these stories became the central part of his search for meaning, for his "soul." He sought as well to understand the way the *mind*, the human psyche, functions. It is important to note that all of the figures in these scenes that he imagined came from his Judeo-Christian culture. It is only later that he will understand the universality of the mythic figures and motifs with which he was engaged in his experiment on his own psyche.

From 1915 until 1929, he copied out these texts, in calligraphy that imitated the writings of monks during the Middle Ages, and painted images to accompany and illustrate them: these are the contents of the Red Book. Along the way, especially during his military service in 1917 during World War II, he began to do drawings in his notebook that he later recognized as mandalas, although he had no consciousness of the significance, the *symbolism*, of the mandala. In 1928, Richard Wilhelm asked Jung to write a commentary on his translation of the Chinese alchemical text "The Secret of the Golden Flower," and Jung was immediately struck by the resemblances between this Eastern philosophy and what he had discerned in his exploration of the way the human psyche functions. Around this time, he abandoned his work on the Red Book itself, and left it unfinished.

Jung decided to keep this book out of the scientific world, fearing that its content would seriously diminish his reputation as a medical man in the West, as a psychiatrist, since the contents read more as delusion than as science. And yet, he was convinced—already one hundred years ago—that western science and Eastern traditions are cut from the same cloth within the human psyche.

After Jung died in 1961, the Red Book remained locked away in a Swiss bank vault until Jung's descendants were convinced by the British historian of analytical psychology, Sonu Shamdasani (clearly of Indian origin!), to allow it to be translated and published. Shamdasani worked on this project for ten years, and the result is this facsimile of Jung's original book, accompanied by an English translation, brilliant footnotes by Shamdasani, and the rest of the text that Jung did not copy into the Red Book. It is with gratitude and in the hope that it will further Mind and Life's mission that Amy and I bring it to you today.

Leslie de Galbert

## NOTES

1. The Mind and Life Institute's website is www.mindandlife.org.

2. The program for the entire five days of the Ecology, Ethics and Interdependence conference can be reviewed on the Mind and Life Institute website.

# FILM REVIEWS

# BUDDHISM, SUFFERING, AND BEING HUMAN
## AKIRA KUROSAWA'S *LOWER DEPTHS*

HELENA BASSIL-MOROZOW

Akira Kurosawa's *Lower Depths* (*Donzoko*, in Japanese) is a bleak study of human nature and human ability to deal with fate, suffering, and social marginality. It is a film about a group of disenfranchised people who dream of a better life and attempt to reclaim some control over their destinies.

*Lower Depths* (1957) is based on the Soviet author Maxim Gorky's play of the same name. Gorky's work is a glimpse into the life of the lower classes in prerevolutionary Russia. Gorky's task was primarily to show the conditions of underprivileged social strata in the fast-developing capitalist society. The play takes place in a tenement house owned by Mikhail Kostyliov and his wife Vassilissa. Their tenants are all impoverished individuals with various miserable backgrounds: a prostitute, a failed actor, a locksmith, a dumpling peddler, a former member of the minor aristocracy, a cap maker, a cobbler, and a thief. They live in one large room—the center stage of their empty, meaningless existence, a stage which sees bitter fighting, poisonous

Helena Bassil-Morozow is a cultural philosopher and film scholar, researching the dynamic between individual personality and sociocultural systems in industrialized and postindustrial societies. She is an honorary research fellow of the Research Institute for Media Art and Design, University of Bedfordshire. Her books include *Tim Burton: The Monster and the Crowd* and *The Trickster in Contemporary Film*.

bickering, death, murder, and suicide. When a new lodger is introduced—a Christian pilgrim called Luka—he attempts to mollify this state of affairs by expressing empathy toward the hapless tenants and by listening to their problems. However, this belated intervention fails to stop any of the disasters from happening: one of the lodgers dies from hunger, neglect, and disease; Vassily, the thief, accidentally kills the landlord; and finally, the alcoholic actor commits suicide.

Kurosawa's version is transposed to Japan of the Edo period (seventeenth to nineteenth centuries), and the names, setting, and religious references are Japanese, yet the screenplay follows Gorky's original. Kurosawa is faithful to the spirit and the narrative of the play. In a 1960 interview with Donald Richie, Kurosawa says:

> Gorky's setting was imperial Russia, but I changed it to Japan, the Edo period. Also I used *bakabayashi* [a kind of music—flute, drums, clappers—traditionally associated with traveling entertainments, shrine fairs, and the annual *matsuri*]. We always think of this music as being joyous and festive. I used it precisely for the opposite reason. I wanted to suggest something tragic and dark.
>
> In Edo during this period the Shogunate was falling to pieces and thousands were living almost unendurable lives. Their resentment we can still feel in *senryu* and *rakushu* [satirical poems and entertainments] of the period. I wanted to show this atmosphere, to reveal it, though whether I really did or no, I don't yet know.[1]

Richie clarifies:

> Kurosawa's choice of period was intended ironically. Most Japanese look back romantically to the Edo period—age of the great courtesans, great Kabuki, great woodcut artists, great literature—with extreme nostalgia. Kurosawa thinks of life at the time as comparable to the miseries in 19th-century Russia.[2]

In the interview Kurosawa also says that he enjoyed working on the film and insists that it was easy to make:

> We worked steadily and well, and shooting did not take long. We had only one closed set, and one open set. We also had many rehearsals, and worked out all the choreography, movements,

camera shots, etc. well in advance. Once, to get everyone in the
proper mood, I invited on to the set one of the few remaining
practitioners of the old Edo *rakugo* [humorous but highly satiric
stories], and we never had more fun than on that day.[3]

The film's mise-en-scène is suitably dim and gloomy. The tenement
is shaky and dilapidated; the bunk beds are dirty and stained; walls,
sliding doors, and partitions are rotten and blackened with soot. The
bunk beds are separated by dirty curtains that look like holed bedsheets.
The floor is barely covered with worn-out rugs and straw. The actors'
costumes are ragged and torn. The mise-en-scène suitably emphasizes
the profound degradation and dehumanization to which the inhabitants
of the flophouse are subjected. Religion is offered as an immaterial way
of dealing with the social ills that have such a conspicuous physical
presence in the film.

## BUDDHISM, SUFFERING, AND THE SOCIAL CONTEXT

In Gorky's play, Luka's profoundly Christian message and his
appeal to their humanity are lost on the inhabitants of the
flophouse—his empathy comes too late, and his religious wisdom,
albeit well-intentioned, is certainly not enough to deal with the social
and political issues that led the characters of the play onto the path
of homelessness, destitution, and crime in the first place. The play
was celebrated in the Soviet Union precisely for the social nature of
Gorky's message: empathy alone cannot solve complex class issues
and social problems. Where suffering is involved, political action is
necessary. Religion is too amorphous, apathetic, and inept to deal
with class problems.

In *Donzoko,* Kurosawa replaces Orthodox Christianity with
Buddhism—and shows that the latter is just as powerless against
poverty, cruelty, disease, alcoholism, and anger. The film argues with
Buddhism about the nature and preventability of suffering. It disagrees
with Buddha's words: "I teach suffering, its origin, cessation and path.
That's all I teach."[4] In fact, the film questions Buddhism's ability to
deal successfully with both emotional or relational problems of human
beings and with the sociopolitical aspect of existence.

Kurosawa replaces Luka the Christian pilgrim with Kahei (played
by Bokuzen Hidari), a Buddhist wanderer and old wise man—but

Buddhist wisdom is manifestly struggling to deal with squalor and misery. Kahei arrives several scenes into the movie and unleashes the tension that has been visibly accumulating in the overcrowded tenement between the inhabitants of the flophouse during the exposition. He acts as a trickster by triggering change and releasing the emotional pressure.

Kahei's trickster qualities (like those of his predecessor, Luka) lie in his therapeutic ability to listen to everyone and to tease out their problems, innermost thoughts, and concerns. He does not have to work too hard on this though—the inhabitants are hungry for human company; they feel lonely, neglected, and abused, surrounded by similarly cruel and inwardly angry people. In the film, degradation and suffering are all-pervasive and no kindness is shown to the tenants by the landlords—Rokubei (played by Ganjirô Nakamura) and his wife Osugi (Isuzu Yamada). However, the tenants themselves have few warm feelings toward their fellow human beings. They make life in the slum unbearable by mocking each other, and abuse spreads like wildfire as the characters try to reclaim some control over their lives by taking away others' self-esteem, self-respect, and basic dignity.

At best, they treat each other as animals, and at worst as disposable objects. For instance, Sutekichi (Toshirô Mifune), the thief, offers to buy a drink for Tonosama (Minoru Chiaki)—the tenant who claims to be a former samurai—but demands that he earn this drink by yelping like a dog. Sutekichi enjoys being the richest man in the tenement and likes to manipulate others, although his manipulation is often done jokingly and warmheartedly. In turn, Tonosama cruelly taunts the prostitute Osen (Akemi Negishi) when she starts inventing escapist stories about romantic men who are interested in her as a person rather than as a sex toy to be bought for money. His rough jokes and taunting conceal his concern for her; they hide sympathy or even a romantic involvement mingled with a degree of jealousy—but he feels too unhappy and degraded himself to take care of another human being. The inhabitants' lives are so tough that there is no place for warmth and emotions in them. Whenever there are emotions in the film, they are mostly negative—envy, greed, jealousy, anger—and are expressed violently and mercilessly.

By contrast, Kahei sees every tenant of the flophouse as a person rather than as an object. He listens to the prostitute's stories; he offers sympathy to the dying Asa (Eiko Miyoshi), the wife of the tinker Tomekichi (Eijirô Tôno); he gives advice to Sutekichi when he is trying to work out the possibility of his future with Okayo (Kyôko Kagawa), the younger sister of Osugi, the landlady. Kahei also attempts to help the alcoholic actor (Kamatari Fujiwara) when the latter complains that he has lost his memory and cannot recall the lines he was going to declaim in Kahei's honor.

Ideally, the old wise man wants the tenants to gather their inner strength and curb their addictions, anger, passions, and desires. The actor is devastated by the disappearance of his memory and by his inability to stop drinking. He hates his own weakness—but cannot deal with it either. Kahei says to him:

> Don't be discouraged. Why don't you get some help? There is a place that cures sick folks like you. And all for free. How would you like to go there? . . . It's at a temple. What is it called . . . It will come back to me soon enough. What matters is that you set your mind to it. . . . Start by cutting back on the booze, and then, once you are cured, you simply turn over a new leaf.

The actor, unsure of the strength of his willpower, wonders if he can really pull it off. Kahei's answer carries the spirit of Buddhist philosophy: "You can do anything once you set your mind to it."

Kahei's aim is to make the actor self-improve and self-reflect—to make him individuate. The task is to make the alcoholic man look inside himself and to teach him to draw the strength from within. Kahei notices the man's weakness and brokenness and attempts to initiate the process of self-healing. He wants the actor to awaken and to renew his life. Richard K. Payne compares Buddhist awakening to the Jungian concept of individuation. Both imply becoming whole:

> In his foreword to D. T. Suzuki's *Introduction to Zen Buddhism*, Jung explains that the "individuation process" is his term for "becoming whole." He then goes on almost immediately to suggest that Zen is committed to the goal of becoming whole as well. J. J. Clarke asserts that Jung was more sympathetic toward Buddhism than other Asian religions, and that one of the reasons for that greater sympathy is that what he found in Buddhism "was a method which was built on the self's capacity and urge to realise itself through its own efforts to seek individuation."[5]

Wholeness, however, is an idealistic goal, and it is not easy to attain—particularly in the circumstances in which the actor lives. Kahei wants the alcoholic man to try and curb his addiction—but somehow the audience senses that the little man, broken by fate, is incapable of saving himself however strong his intentions are to do so. Kahei implies that the "temple" that helps alcoholics is not real—it is imaginary, metaphorical, spiritual—it is an internal temple. However, in order to do access this temple inside one's soul, one must have enough willpower and a degree of resilience.

Eric Mazur notes that in *Donzoko* Kurosawa's skeptical (and quixotic) humanism is overtaken by despair at the fallen state of humanity, the brevity of life, and the inexorable workings of fate (or karma).[6] The notion of karma is closely related to social ills in the film. The prostitute, the actor, the impoverished samurai, and the dying wife of the tinker are all helpless against fate. The choice offered by Buddhism—and by Kahei as its representative—is to accept the suffering, or dissatisfaction, which is seen by Buddhist philosophy as part of the delusion that is individualism. Suffering is only a subjective experience based on one's perception of oneself as separate from the world—as being an individual entitled to better things in life. Kahei does not aspire to stage a revolution—he attempts to teach a group of angry, hungry, miserable, afflicted people how to accept physical and emotional pain, unjust social conditions, and any other blows of karma quietly and honorably.

David R. Loy, a specialist in Japanese Zen Buddhism, writes that

> the fundamental insight of Buddhism is the connection it emphasizes between [suffering] and the self: "My deepest frustration is caused by my sense of being a self that is separate from the world I am in. This sense of separation is illusory—in fact, it is our most dangerous delusion."[7]

But there is another issue: the personal self (and this is very much a Jungian idea) is closely related to the collective self and is therefore inseparable from the collective karma: "If there are collective selves, does that mean there are also collective greed, collective ill will, collective delusion?"[8] In other words, if the personal is so inseparable from the social, the whole issue of karma takes on a social hue.

Neither Gorky's play nor Kurosawa's film provide the audience with insight into the characters' personal and social backgrounds. We don't know why Osen became a prostitute, what turned the actor into an alcoholic, or how the samurai lost his wealth. The implication is, however, that their hapless existence is the result of a combination of social misfortunes and personal weaknesses. Asa, the tinker's wife, is dying because she is malnourished and physically infirm. She dreams of being able to "eat her fill"—something she has never had. She accepts her suffering meekly and passively, unlike the other inhabitants of the tenement who bitterly grumble about being treated unfairly by the fate.

What Kurosawa questions here is Buddhism's ability to deal with basic human weaknesses alongside the social ills that make them worse. In his encouraging speech to the actor, the old wise man propagates one of the key postulates of Buddhism, namely, that the root of suffering is desire and that the task of human beings is to curb their desires. Kahei personally demonstrates his lack of desire for worldly pleasures when he says that any warm spot will do "for an old geezer like me." He does not expect life to offer him more than just a temporary place in a ramshackle tenement. He accepts any small offerings from the fate with gratitude. He is humble. By contrast, the actor is suffering because he aspired to a successful career on stage, and when his career went downhill, he despaired. His ambitions are now in ruins—but the memory of acceptance and love haunts him. He is plagued by desires as he has obsessive nature.

## THE INDIVIDUAL'S ILLUSION OF CONTROL

At the end of the film the actor commits suicide, thus creating the second and final climax. He does not have much control over his life, and ending it all is the only decision he is free to make. This decision is his attempt to reclaim some control over his existence. By committing suicide, he becomes an agent rather than a passive, powerless creature tossed about by all forms of authority—from the greedy landlords to the vagaries of luck. By committing suicide, he also gets rid of the overwhelming sense of shame that comes with feeling unwanted and unloved.

Buddhism is essentially nonheroic as its aim is to dispel the delusion of proactive human beings able to change and to challenge the world. As it regards separateness from the world as an illusion, the individual's control over the world is only an illusion of control. This means that the individual has to deal with shame and the feeling of being small and insignificant; with the inability to influence external events, with being unloved, rejected, or neglected by others. These feelings are universal because the entirety of reality, according to Buddhist wisdom, is the realm of delusion.[9]

The sense of shame is born simultaneously with the realization of the need to protect oneself from the public eye—with the realization of the difference between "I" and "them," with the idea of an autonomous self separate from the rest of the world. The birth of the individual is the birth of shame. The Bible takes the loss of paradisiacal infant omnipotence as the base for what it means to be human. The biblical story of Adam and Eve places shame at the heart of human experience: we are born out of self-recognition, out of experiencing the world as "other," as different; out of the realization that others exist separately from us.

The individualistic/heroic mood—the normal psychological state of the Western individual—arrives with this separateness. An individual feels that he or she must attain personal achievements. The emphasis is on developing a personality that is separate from the community emotionally, financially, and psychologically. In an article titled "Promises and Perils of the Spiritual Path," Jack Engler writes that Western people often confuse Buddhist enlightenment with individualist striving for perfection:

> Enlightenment can be imagined as a heaven-sent embodiment of a core western narcissistic ideal: a state of personal perfection from which all of our badness, all our faults and defilements have been expelled, a state in which we will finally become self-sufficient, not needing anyone or anything, above criticism and reproach, and above all, immune to further hurts and disappointments. Practice can be motivated in part by this secret wish to be special, if not superior: enlightenment will finally elicit the knowledge and admiration that have been lacking.[10]

In heroic mentalities, failure to be the best is associated with shame and lack of control. Shame is also part of the process of seeing oneself as separate from one's surroundings. Shame is about connecting, making contact with the alien others. When faced with the irreversible difference and foreign nature of the world, we become intent on establishing ourselves in it and on making our impression on our surroundings. People need to conquer, seduce, lure, and—when all else fails—manipulate and threaten the world into understanding us, because if we do not, our sense of shame will remind us about our loneliness and lack of visible, recognizable, strong, resilient, acceptable, and loveable individuality. Being accepted and being loved reduces the sense of shame in human beings because it covers the gap between the private and the public, between self and other, between I and Thou. It is as if the world becomes the mirror reflecting the self's desires and thoughts, reflecting one's inner core, thereby confirming one's existence as an individual.

Shame is relieved by mirroring. When surrounded by like-minded people, we feel safe, understood, cared for. We feel omnipotent, in charge of things. Mario Jacoby quotes the writer Georges Simenon talking about the correlation between shame and mirroring: "Everyone has a shadow side of which he is more or less ashamed. But when I see someone who resembles me, who shares the same symptoms, the same shame, the same inner battles, then I say to myself, so I am not alone in this, I am no monster."[11]

Unlike guilt, which presupposes the feeling of being in control, albeit negatively, shame is a deeper feeling associated with being out of control, being helpless, disarmed as an agent. Jacoby writes that

> It may be less painful to search for what caused the relationship to break up than to imagine that one simply was not attractive or sexy enough. If a person does not simply escape the pain by blaming the other, he may prefer to think of the times that he was guilty of hurting, abandoning, and treating his lovers insensitively. Confessions of guilt also hold out the hope that mistakes will be rectified, all will be forgiven. But the feeling that one is personally unworthy of love cuts much deeper.[12]

In Buddhism, the individual—separate from the world—does not exist, there is no "I," no (Jungian) ego or (Winnicottian) self. The whole shame-control dichotomy is as delusional as the concept of individuality, which supposedly originates in them. Kahei's task is to deliver the characters from shame as well as from the desire to control their fate, which he sees as delusional and unnecessary. For him, it is the root of all their troubles. The concept of control is central to the understanding of the play and the film. It is this need for control, which is accompanied by shame and the humiliating feeling of being a nobody, of being socially and personally insignificant, that leads to all the bickering and fighting between the characters.

### KARMA AS AUTHORITY

The inhabitants of the flophouse can be subdivided into three groups according to their reaction to the sense of powerlessness. They all deal differently with the supremacy of authority, which for them is a combination of factors including past events that caused their present misery and destitution, the heartless landlords, and the political and economic situation.

The first group is comprised of the actor, the prostitute, and the samurai. They are the most exposed and fragile of the inhabitants, symbolizing the frailty of human existence. All three are pushed by cruel fate into a state of physical and moral degradation. They are used to this degradation and yet they feel angry and vulnerable; they have difficulty accepting their fallen state in a true Buddhist way. All three had a lot to lose: the actor lost his memory and job; the prostitute lost her physical and moral integrity as well as faith in the goodness of human beings; and the samurai lost his lifestyle. The only adequate way to deal with the feeling of being exposed and helpless is to escape the world of reality and flee into the realm of fantasy and illusion. The actor drowns his shame in alcohol, the prostitute escapes by inventing stories about true love, and the samurai lies about his affluent past. They all reminisce or lie about times when they were loved and needed by others: by the public, by a romantic and caring man, or by a feudal lord. The loss of social position brings about feelings so strong that these characters' internal and external reactions are extreme and violent.

The second group consists of the people who are able to find alternative—or roundabout—ways of feeling superior. They are the clever ones. Yoshisaburo (Kôji Mitsui), the gambler, and Sutekichi, the thief—the two crooks—regain a sense of control by rejecting and duping authority. As a result, they feel slightly better than the honest characters—they feel smug and confident because they are able to fool the system. Sutekichi is the former lover of Osugi, the landlady, but has recently fallen in love with her more virtuous younger sister, Okayo. Osugi becomes jealous and does everything she can to spoil Okayo's life. She regularly beats her up and at one point even pours a bucket of hot water over her legs, causing severe burns.

Sutekichi intends to marry Okayo, find a proper job, and move out of the tenement. Osugi, who hates her old husband Rokubei, is not pleased with this plan. She wants Sutekichi to kill Rokubei. Sutekichi does not agreed with this idea, but he ends up killing Rokubei by accident and going to prison. His project of controlling his life and escaping karma fails.

The way of the third group is that of proactive hope, adopted by Tomekichi, the tinker, and Otaki (Nijiko Kiyokawa), the candy seller. Otaki goes out to work every day, and she does not feel put off by the sight of the other unhappy, heavily drinking inhabitants. She keeps doing her own thing despite of the demotivating climate. Other inhabitants of the flophouse both respect her optimism and laugh at it. Her strategy proves to be correct because she becomes the new owner of the tenement when Osugi and Sutekichi are arrested for the murder of Rokubei. On the other hand, it can be argued that Otaki's success is a random event and has nothing to do with her hard work or determination. Her success is due to the trickster chance rather than actions. This is confirmed in the film by the fact that the tinker also works hard but does not have any luck. He hammers away all day mending household utensils and still has no money. He is so miserable and downtrodden that he has no space left in his heart for emotions. His neglected and sickly wife dies, and Yoshisaburo, the gambler, laughs at his determination to earn his living by hard and fair work.

Instead of accepting the challenges stoically and wisely—like the wise Buddhist pilgrim Kahei does—the characters become desperate, bitter, and terrified. Their bottled-up anger and exasperation find expression in ludic, hysterical forms—for instance, when Kuna (Atsushi Watanabe), the local trickster and madman, runs into the tenement and starts shouting, singing, and dancing frantically. Kuna epitomizes everyone else's hatred of the landlords when he shouts rude jokes about Osugi and her husband. When Osugi arrives, threatens him, and attempts to throw him out, he cries out that he has nothing to lose and that she can cut him into strips—he is not scared of her or of anyone.

The other ludic happening involves everyone: sometimes the inhabitants of the flophouse start singing and dancing all together. Usually this happens during their collective drinking sessions. They even draw in the sullen tartar nursing the wounded arm that prevents him from working. This *bakabayashi*-style entertainment—alongside alcohol—are the only pleasures accessible to them. Collective singing of sad songs brings them together and keeps them physically and psychologically alive. During these moments of hysterical cooperation and paradoxical friendliness they feel relief from their emotional burden. In a way, it is as therapeutic as their conversations with Kahei. However, singing and dancing cannot cure the social ills displayed in the film: in the last scene their merrymaking is interrupted by the news, delivered by Osen the prostitute, of the actor's suicide. Their singing is nothing but escapism—an attempt to forget their tragic and empty existence.

Keiko McDonald notes that Kurosawa is a moralist "eager to persuade us that society can be improved by individuals motivated by compassion. Obviously, his view of morality is deeply rooted in Buddhism. But Kurosawa's morality insists on a measure of social and political activism."[13] In *Donzoko* Kurosawa insists that Buddhism fails to deal with social and political issues as it offers no proactive solutions and does not intend to reform the system or challenge authority. It is not that Kahei's skill as a therapist is not required in this kind of society, but it comes too late, when most of these people are already morally and emotionally dead, and it is certainly not sufficient. Kahei's therapeutic ways of dealing with the characters' issues—listening to them and giving them advice—cannot replace practical solutions to poverty, prostitution, alcoholism, illness, and physical and emotional abuse. The failure of the Buddhist solution is further emphasized by the fact that Kahei runs away when the real trouble happens—when Rokubei is killed by Sutekichi—because he is scared of appearing as a witness at court. This might mean, of course, that Kahei has something to hide, and yet this demonstrates the old wise man's failure to attend to the practical side of the situation. He also cannot remember the name of the temple where monks could help the actor deal with his affliction. It is no coincidence that Kahei disappears during the film's climatic moment, when his help is acutely required by the characters and he can possibly save Sutekichi from life in prison. The Buddhist solution offered by Kahei to the people living in squalor—that is, putting up with the hard blows of fate and embracing everything that comes their way stoically and wisely—is unacceptable for Kurosawa.

## NOTES

1. Donald Richie, "A Personal Record: Kurosawa and I," in *Akira Kurosawa: Interviews,* ed. Bert Cardullo (Jackson, MS: University Press of Mississippi, 2008), p. 16.

2. *Ibid.*

3. *Ibid.*

4. "The Four Noble Truths," BBC Religions: Buddhism, n.d., accessed at http://www.bbc.co.uk/religion/religions/buddhism/beliefs/fournobletruths_1.shtml.

5. Richard K. Payne, "Individuation and Awakening: Romantic Narrative and the Psychological Interpretation of Buddhism," in *Buddhism and Psychotherapy across Cultures: Essays on Theories and Practices,* ed. Mark Unno (Somerville, MA: Wisdom Publications, 2006), p. 33.

6. Eric Michael Mazur, *Encyclopaedia of Religion and Film* (Santa Barbara, CA: ABC-CLIO, 2011), p. 282.

7. David R. Loy, *Money, Sex, War, Karma: Notes for a Buddhist Revolution* (Somerville, MA: Wisdom Publications, 2008), p. 89.

8. *Ibid.*, p. 90.

9. Naito Chiko, "Shinran's Thought Regarding Birth in the Pure Land," in *Buddhism and Psychotherapy across Cultures,* p. 276.

10. Jack Engler, "Promises and Perils of the Spiritual Path," in *Buddhism and Psychotherapy across Cultures,* p. 25.

11. Mario Jacoby, *Shame and the Origins of Self-Esteem* (London: Routledge, 1991), p. xi.

12. *Ibid.*, p. 2.

13. Keiko I. McDonald, *Reading a Japanese Film: Cinema in Context* (Honolulu: University of Hawai'i Press, 2006), p. 46.

# WERNER HERZOG'S *WHEEL OF TIME*

CATRIONA MILLER

*W heel of Time* (2003) is a documentary by renowned film director Werner Herzog. It is largely concerned with depicting the Tibetan Buddhist Kalachakra ritual, held (in this instance) by the Dalai Lama in 2002, in Bodh Gaya, India, and then in Graz in Austria. *Kalachakra* means "Wheel of Time."[1] It focuses on twelve days of preparation and ritual during which Buddhist monks make a mandala representing the Kalachakra deity and students are initiated into the universe of enlightenment represented by the highly complex mandala. Herzog was given "exclusive interviews with the Dalai Lama, [and] access to secret rituals for the first time on film."[2]

It is outside the scope of a review of this sort to discuss in any detail the influence that Buddhist thought might have had on the development of Jung's ideas, but there are perhaps some interesting touch points between Herzog's documentary, Buddhism, and Jung that can be discussed. Jung was very interested in other cultures, albeit cautiously so, and he traveled to India in 1937–1938, where he visited the Stupa of Sanchi, which he described in *Memories, Dreams, Reflections*, recalling the intensity of emotion the visit evoked.

Catriona Miller, Ph.D., is a senior lecturer at Glasgow Caledonian University, where she teaches film theory and writing for television. Her research interests include the archetypal dimensions of science fiction, horror, and fantasy genres, and she has published in Jungian film and television studies in *Jung and Film 2* (2012) and *House: The Wounded Healer on Television* (2011). Her website is www.gcu.ac.uk/gsbs/staff/drcatrionamiller.

"For Jung, the East was a mirror in which the West could find wisdom for its much-needed self-awareness," although he was "determined not to become a slavish disciple of Eastern wisdom."[3] As he suggested in the foreword to D. T. Suzuki's book *An Introduction to Zen Buddhism*,

> this author does venture to say of enlightenment that it embraces an insight into the nature of self, and that it is an emancipation of the conscious from an illusionary conception of self. The illusion regarding the nature of self is the common confusion of the ego with self.[4]

Jung understood enlightenment as a transformative psychic experience, arising from the unconscious and experienced as "the unexpected, comprehensive, completely illuminating answer, which operates all the more as illumination and revelation, since the conscious has wedged itself into a hopeless blind alley."[5] However, it is worth noting that Jung's interest in Buddhism, his trip to India notwithstanding, seems to have been based rather more in the Zen Buddhist tradition than in the Tibetan one. (Some comments regarding yogic and meditative practice toward the end of the foreword suggest that he did not entirely approve of the more "exotic" elements of yogic Buddhist practice, at least as a method for Westerners.)

Herzog, too, appears to maintain a certain caution or distance from the rituals he is filming, though perhaps this is only his filmmaking technique at play. Elsaesser suggests that it is (as an example of *Verfremdung* [defamiliarization]) "a stupid eye, one that is merely curious rather than knowing or demonstrative."[6] Herzog certainly does not offer much in the way of context or explanation for the images he presents. After a brief mention of Siddhartha Gautama at the beginning, Herzog offers no account of Buddhism in general or of Tibetan Buddhism in particular, nor does he speak about the politics of Tibet. He briefly mentions the traditional Tibetan Bon religion, which influenced many of the practices of Tibetan Buddhism, during the Mount Kailash sequence, but he does not offer an explanation of the philosophy underlying the Kalachakra ritual or indeed even the techniques intended to foster enlightenment in that context.

Herzog is certainly not an uncritical admirer of Tibetan Buddhism—he does not hide the elements of superstition that might sit a little uncomfortably with his (presumably) Western audiences. For example, he shows the Dalai Lama consulting with an oracle toward the end of the film, and an earlier sequence he shows pilgrims rubbing themselves against a pillar believed to have healing properties. Even his interview with the Dalai Lama is surprisingly casual. When asked about the importance of Mount Kailash, the Dalai Lama explains that everybody thinks their own country is the center of the universe, but in fact each individual person is the center of the universe. Werner replies that this makes him feel very good . . . but he shouldn't tell his wife. It is a distinctly awkward moment, and in the later sequence set in Austria, one writer makes the point that the Dalai Lama is positioned rather more as a celebrity than a religious leader.[7] However, Herzog is never a deferential filmmaker.

## HERZOG THE DIRECTOR

Herzog has been making films since 1968, often (though not exclusively) outside the Hollywood system, and he is a director with a distinctive filmmaking voice, both literally and figuratively, engaging personally with each subject and topic. Thus this documentary is not about the politics of the region or the person of the Dalai Lama, nor is it an explanation of the tenets of Tibetan Buddhism. Rather, in keeping with Herzog's wider oeuvre, "Herzog wants to document the fascination that emanates from the fictional or fantastic elements at the very heart of the everyday occurrence."[8] In this case, a ritual in the Tibetan Buddhist tradition.

Herzog's mode of filmmaking attempts to access the internal world of the psyche through the external pictures his films offer, seeking to depict the embodiment of the spiritual in the audiovisual texts he creates. As one writer suggests, Herzog's style of depicting landscapes in particular claims "to visualize the inner world of the emotions, the psyche, and the soul—vast areas of human experience that are not directly observable and therefore tend to be ignored by scholars of documentary."[9] These are not the truths that documentary usually tries to depict, but perhaps it is a problem that Jung might have found familiar in attempting to do something similar though the language of psychology.

One of the interesting points about this film, and much of Herzog's other work, is an unwillingness to mark out strict boundaries between documentary and fiction modes of working. The idea of seeking to visualize the inner world of the soul in an external medium is not a new one, but it is not, as Ames suggests, something that a *documentary* filmmaker normally tackles. However, like many of the other filmmakers that emerged from the new German cinema of the 1970s, Herzog's documentary films cannot be seen in isolation from his fiction films, and as far as Herzog is concerned truth and fiction are closely related. In his Minnesota Declaration (1999), he stated: "There are deeper strata of truth in cinema, and there is such a thing as poetic, ecstatic truth. It is mysterious and elusive, and can be reached only through fabrication and imagination and stylization."[10]

This stylization means that Herzog's documentaries are never simply a factual retelling of some event or the biography of an individual. They are, in fact, very much *his* documentaries, *his* selection of images and sounds. The director's fingerprints are all over his work. Whether factual or fiction, what the audience sees is his vision and what they hear is his voice (which has become a stylistic hallmark in its own right—Peter Bradshaw, at the *Guardian*, called it "unmistakable.")[11] Herzog is "a director who heightens the documentary stance to the point where it becomes itself a powerful fiction," and it would be safe to say that Herzog's documentaries require the audience to remain alert to his tall tales, possibly taking pleasure in their ludic qualities and forcing them to engage in their own interpretation of what he offers.[12] These are not the predigested meanings of the Hollywood mode.

### Ecstasy and Embodiment in *Wheel of Time*

However, what of the "deeper strata of truth" and "ecstatic truth" of which he speaks? As already noted, in *Wheel of Time* Herzog is not interested in explaining the Kalachakra initiation in the way one might expect. The film opens with long lingering shots of the Indo-Ganges Plain and the story of Siddhartha Gautama finding enlightenment under a tree before introducing the village of Bodh Gaya, where the initiation is to take place, and the mandala that forms the center of the initiation ritual. Herzog quickly describes the mandala as "depiction of an inner landscape," before the Dalai Lama himself states: "The main thing is visualization, not external mandala, but internal mandala." Herzog makes it clear from the start that the film it is an attempt to explore a sacred landscape but one that exists both in "functional reality" and in "inner reality."

This is something that Herzog understands well. In an interview he said: "For me, a true landscape is not just a representation of a desert or a forest. It shows an inner state of mind, literally inner landscapes, and it is the human soul that is visible through the landscapes presented in my films."[13] In *Wheel of Time* he takes the audience from the mandala to an extended sequence centered around a pilgrimage to Mount Kailash. "Since the mandala forms a kind of map of an inner landscape, a vision of a sacred cosmography, we were intrigued to visit the holiest of physical landscapes for Buddhists, Mount Kailash," which he describes elsewhere as "a unique landscape drama full of hieroglyphic mystery."[14]

The film lingers on the landscape around Mount Kailash, a bare landscape of rock and water, pristine and timeless, which seems to sit upon the edge of the known world (echoing the fabled Shangri-la, at least as it exists in Western imagination). But although *Wheel of Time*, like many of Herzog's films, makes an almost expressionist use of landscape, he also presents very embodied human beings. The pilgrims to Mount Kailash are shown at some length laboriously making their way toward the mountain in a series of full-length prostrations, including the awkward task of crossing a river without getting wet. Back at the ceremony in Bodh Gaya, Herzog also interviews a serene-looking monk who had traveled more than three thousand miles by such a method. His forehead still bears the marks of being pressed to the ground and the bones of his hands have grown bony nodes. These pilgrims are directly, physically engaged with the landscape through which they progress, and Herzog appears to respect the pilgrims and admires the extent of their devotional practices, as he has admired the intensity of actor Klaus Kinski and a host of other obsessive eccentrics who have appeared in his films over the years.

There are many scenes of pilgrims and monks making their devotions, seeking blessings, meditating and debating; however, Herzog's films always contain a certain dry wit, and while not diminishing the ecstatic devotional images he offers, he also cannot resist a look behind the scenes, at the kitchens, for example, suggesting perhaps just a little irreverence but showing the very humanness of what is going on. One sequence includes scenes of devotion but also younger monks running here and there to distribute tea from huge cauldrons while it is still hot, boy monks laughing, chipmunks eating scraps, and a man with a dancing monkey. He also shows a less spiritual sequence where monks distributing gifts for the Long Life ceremony have the baskets deliberately pulled from their hands, their gifts spilled on the ground and the pilgrims scrambling to grab as much as possible. Herzog makes the point that even in the midst of a ceremony designed to stimulate enlightenment, the faithful do not escape the embodied nature of their experience.

Herzog's filmmaking task may be an impossible one. He is trying to show an internal transformation externally on physical film, *Wheel of Time*, and as such must hold in tension both the reality of embodied physicality and his conceptions of the ecstatic and sublime. And the film is not entirely successful insofar as there is no resolution. The culminating moments of the initiation ceremony, when they finally arrive, are rather anticlimactic, with Herzog's soft voice commenting that after many hours of meditation and purification, "a culminating spiritual event invisible for our camera thus comes to an end." There are no visible signs offered as to whether the spiritual transformation occurred or at least whether the (Western) pilgrims were satisfied, and Herzog does not interview any of the pilgrims after the initiation to seek their views. Instead he shows the destruction of the mandala, and then turns the camera back to Bodh Gaya and a lone monk still meditating among "400,000 empty pillows." Referring back to an earlier comment by the Dalai Lama, Herzog wonders if *this* is the center of the universe.

However, with the very final images of the film, Herzog cannot resist a return to his "sacred landscape full of hieroglyphic mystery"—Mount Kailash. Rather than seeing Eastern spiritual practice as a route to self-awareness, it is tempting to suggest that Herzog is more impressed with the *landscapes* of the East, but this would be erroneous on two counts. It is not simply the landscape of the East that attracts Herzog but *all* landscapes, though one might say he does harbor a preference for the periphery (deserts, mountains, jungles). Second, these final shots of Mount Kailash and environs are not intended as an appeal for some kind of cosmological meaning, for

Herzog does not subscribe to an idealized or sentimental understanding of nature. "Herzog wants his landscapes to talk back to us and to the figures that populate them, yet from his point of view they have nothing to express but their wholesale indifference."[15] Perhaps Herzog would agree with Jung:

> Every spiritual happening is a picture and an imagination; were this not so, there could be no consciousness and no phenomenality of the occurrence. The imagination itself is a psychic occurrence, and therefore whether an "enlightenment" is called "real" or "imaginary" is quite immaterial.[16]

Herzog's real interest remains in *process* rather than in result. In an interview about *Wheel of Time* he said, "I had a physical curiosity to depict spirituality, and it can be done on film."[17] A typically audacious objective for Herzog, though, of course, in the end its success can be judged only by the audience.

## NOTES

1. For more detail see, for example, K. Pandell and B. Bryant, *Learning from the Dalai Lama: Secrets of the Wheel of Time* (New York: Dutton, 1995).

2. "Wheel of Time," accessed November 15, 2012, at http://www.wernerherzog.com/114.html.

3. P. Young-Eisendrath and S. Muramoto, *Awakening and Insight: Zen Buddhism and Psychotherapy* (London: Bunner-Routledge, 2002), p. 127; S. Walker, *Jung and the Jungians on Myth* (New York: Routledge, 2002), p. 85.

4. C. G. Jung, foreword to D. T. Suzuki, *An Introduction to Zen Buddhism* (New York: Grove Press, 1964), p. xiii.

5. *Ibid.*, pp. xxiii–xxiv.

6. T. Elsaesser, *New German Cinema: A History* (New Brunswick, NJ: Rutgers University Press, 1989), p. 166.

7. B. Prager, *The Cinema of Werner Herzog* (London: Wallflower Press, 2007), p. 85.

8. Elsaesser, *New German Cinema*, pp. 165–166.

9. E. Ames, *Ferocious Reality: Documentary According to Werner Herzog* (Minneapolis: University of Minnesota Press, 2012), p. 50.

10. Article 5 of the Minnesota Declaration, accessed at http://www.wernerherzog.com/52.html#c93.

11. Peter Bradshaw, "Cave of Forgotten Dreams—Review," *Guardian*, March 24, 2011, accessed at http://www.guardian.co.uk/film/2011/mar/24/cave-of-forgotten-dreams-review.

12. Elsaesser, *New German Cinema*, p. 165.

13. Paul Cronin, ed., *Herzog on Herzog* (London: Faber and Faber, 2002), p. 136.

14. Lena Herzog and Werner Herzog, *Pilgrim: Becoming the Path Itself* (London: Periplus Publishing, 2004), p. 14.

15. Prager, *The Cinema of Werner Herzog*, p. 14.

16. Jung, in Suzuki, *An Introduction to Zen Buddhism*, p. xv.

17. E. Ames, "Herzog, Landscape and Documentary," in *Cinema Journal* 48, no. 2 (Winter 2009): 60.

# BOOK REVIEWS

# BOOK REVIEWS

Deborah Bowman, *The Female Buddha: Discovering the Heart of Liberation and Love* (Boulder, CO: Samadhi Publications, 2012).

### REVIEWED BY PATRICIA REIS

D eborah Bowman begins her introduction to this lavishly illustrated book with what Jungians call a big dream:

> I was walking in a large English garden in which there were three towering figures of female Buddhas carved out of stone. Each was over 100 feet tall sitting peacefully in meditation. In awe, I walked between them on quiet carefully tended pathways. The wonder and serenity I felt in the presence of these majestic figures are indelible in my memory. (p. 8)

This prescient dream arrived at a time of great inner and outer turmoil in her life. Bowman, a transpersonal psychologist who has studied and practiced Buddhism, understood the magnitude of spiritual depth emanating from this towering trinity. She does not attempt to analyze the dream beyond saying it was a necessary compensation, bringing

Patricia Reis is a writer and psychotherapist practicing in Portland, Maine, and Nova Scotia. She is the author of *Daughters of Saturn: From Father's Daughter to Creative Women* and *The Dreaming Way: Dreams and Art for Remembering and Recovery*, available at www.springjournalandbooks.com.

inner balance to her personal psyche. The dream also brought awareness of a collective imbalance; the peace, wisdom, gentle strength, refuge, and love embodied as female signified the very qualities kept in the background as Buddhism wended its way from East to West. The dream became a spiritual landmark, giving direction to her journey.

Bowman first encountered the female Buddha in the form of Guanyin in Vietnam, where she traveled with her husband, a Vietnam War veteran, on a trip of reparation, healing, and meditation practice. Over the course of the next seventeen years, she continued her pilgrimages, searching for Guanyin, the female Buddha, in Bangkok, Thailand, Japan, South Korea, Taiwan, and Myanmar.

A gifted photographer with a sensitive eye, Bowman's visual images are at the heart of the 128-page book. Sculptural images of Guanyin range from monumental to intimate; the women devotees she photographed, laywomen and nuns, are all ages. My favorites are a smiling, saffron-robed nun from Thailand exchanging devotional gazes with a monastery dog as she tenderly places her hand on his head. Another is of an elderly Vietnamese woman seated in repose inside a temple courtyard; a small blue towel drapes her head, a bamboo hat is by her side, and a timeless expression of warmth radiates from her open face. The photographs are accompanied by pith teachings from exceptional women dating from the Buddha's time to the present. Many of the names are familiar, including the Nobel Peace Prize recipient from Myanmar, Aung San Suu Kyi. *The Female Buddha* is a record of Bowman's quest and is wonderfully personal, thoughtful, and inclusive in scope, but not without its challenges.

The book begins with a single quote from a contemporary female teacher from Taiwan, Master Wu Yin, "Being a great human being is not related to gender, it depends on caring about the well-being of all our fellow sentient beings." This quote about gender transcendence opens the door to Bowman's seventeen-page introduction where she tackles some hotly contested issues within the American Buddhist community.

As Bowman notes, during the past century the transmission of Buddhism from East to West came through Asian male teachers and writers and masculine images of Buddhism, despite the fact that, as she discovered in her travels, the face of Buddhism in large parts of

East Asia is also depicted as female. Not only that, but in the countries she visited women practitioners far outnumbered the men she encountered; nuns make up the majority of monastics, and nuns and laywomen provide the material support for most Buddhist activities, including temple, educational, and hospital facilities. Bowman's dream vision, her subsequent travels in Asia, and her meetings with women devoted to Guanyin, whom Asian women refer to as the "lady Buddha," inspired the book. Bowman offers her work with a desire to awaken Western practitioners of all religions to what she calls the universal "feminine qualities" of gentleness and strength, compassion and freedom.

Bowman provides a brief history of the evolution of Kwan Yin, preferring to use her Chinese name, Guanyin. When Buddhism entered China in the second century it was accompanied by the Indian male icon of compassion, the bodhisattva, Avalokiteśvara, with his thousand eyes and arms that perceived suffering and offered succor to those in need. In the eighth century he changed form, and Guanyin, "the one who hears the cries of the world," (re)emerged as female.

I say re-emerged as I suspect there was an indigenous, pre-Buddhist female predecessor to Avalokiteśvara/Guanyin. The evolution of deities in myth and legend from more ancient female ones is a common phenomenon. For example, the prehistoric goddesses of Old Europe connected to the female mysteries of life, death, and rebirth later became hybridized as consorts and virgins in Greek mythology while retaining attributes of their earlier power. So too does Guanyin retain remnants of her more ancient past as the lotus-goddess, the lotus being a primordial symbol of the vulva and the generative powers of water and mud. Perhaps this is consciously or unconsciously part of her appeal.

In Guanyin's iconography, a willow branch she holds or an animal such as a dragon or lion on which she sits or stands indicates her primal ties to nature and instinctual energy. Unlike the more prominent temple Buddhas, Guanyin's placement is typically found in homes, at the entrances of temples, in caves, children's cemeteries, or, as in Bowman's dream, a garden setting. Her wide popularity with women creates a special world of devotional practices; some of Bowman's photographs show women offering lotus blossoms along with their petitions for healing, fertility, and children's well-being. These practices can make Guanyin appear more folk goddess than representative of abstract spiritual attainment.

It is well known that a culture that reveres divine female imagery offers no guarantee that their women will be valued. In fact, Bowman is quick to note that many of the Guanyin devotees she met and observed were women without full access to traditional positions of religious authority: poor laywomen or nuns living in impoverished monasteries. As a more accessible source of refuge, healing, and compassion, similar to the Virgin Mary, Guanyin's heart-centered attributes of benevolence, mercy, and love make her a preeminently maternal figure, one particularly attentive to women's needs. But unlike Mary, Guanyin is not considered an intercessor or go-between in the relations of humans and a male father god; as a female bodhisattva, an enlightened being who forgoes nirvana for the sake of relieving suffering for all, she has the power and the buck can stop with her.

In the West, no figure is more contested than that of mother. We are all "of woman born" as the poet Adrienne Rich said; all humans have passed through a woman's body to attain existence and in her capacity as birth-giver, we call that woman mother. How we engage with this mortal truth, whether we revere or revile, praise or blame, elevate or subjugate this woman is not only a matter of personal history but also of our cultural and religious conditioning. Christianity, for instance, split the mother into Mary, the sexually untainted mother of God, and Eve, the sexually cursed mother of all humans. Western psychological theories with their Judeo-Christian underpinnings have followed suit, placing the blame for our ills firmly on the altar of the mother. Our conscious or unconscious ambivalence, fear, and hostility toward actual mother figures and by extension toward all perceptions of women's power undoubtedly have their basis in our earliest experiences of profound vulnerability and dependence on our first caretaker. The desire for an idealized, if not romanticized, mother with the attributes of unconditional love, one who offers protection, solace, and compassion for our pain, is at the root of our deep longing for a mother liberated from such conflicts.

Why does Guanyin not have breasts? In her iconography, the only female signifier is the veil she wears. Bowman acknowledges that the

> asexual ideal of the mother, expressed in the common form of
> Guanyin without breasts, matches a worldwide characterization
> of woman as saint versus woman as whore . . . . In these sexless

> depictions we observe the cultural preference towards an
> absolute ideal at the expense of our experience as physically
> embodied beings. (p. 11)

Unlike Christianity, Buddhism, especially Tibetan, does not shun highly sexualized female deities, as evidenced by the one image of Tara included in the book, a full-breasted, powerfully sexual image. Bowman notes that images of Guanyin in a more womanly form are beginning to appear, and she quips, "Guanyin is growing up and so are we." Outside of monotheistic religions, a deity can shape-shift to serve certain cultural needs. Change in form implies a change in meaning. What would it mean for this maternal female Buddha to have breasts? What would have to change?

Confusion arises in Bowman's introduction, primarily to do with Buddhist ideals of the absolute, such as gender transcendence, and the relative world in which women face hard realities in their engagement with these spiritual practices. This confusion is illustrated by Bowman's quote from the preeminent feminist Buddhist scholar Rita Gross: "Even in some Buddhist cultures, which posit a very strong ethic of caring in the bodhisattva ideal, in practical, everyday ways, nurturing and caring for relationships are low priorities compared to practicing meditation and studying dharma texts." Bowman responds to this statement by asking, "Isn't selflessness, a quality to be realized through study and meditation, not put to the ultimate test in our ability to care for other beings? Is service not an equally essential training ground for enlightenment?" (p.12) Pondering this exchange, I realize that both women are talking about valuing the deeply relational work of women, mothers and nonmothers alike. Both women protest and resist ranking women's devotion lower on the hierarchy of consciousness. The distance between spiritual absolutes and women's reality, between theory and praxis, is a measure of the distance Buddhists have yet to go.

In the 1970s and '80s, along with the rise of the women's movement in the West, numerous women were drawn to Buddhism for its lack of a dominating father god and its offer of an equal chance at enlightenment. More than half of the women who are quoted in this book are contemporary Western Buddhist scholars, writers, teachers, translators, nuns, physicians, priests, activists, and founders of retreat centers and abbeys. Most have risen through the ranks of

Asian male teachers and have been deeply engaged for years in significant thinking and writing about the relationship of women to Buddhist thought and practice, thereby influencing the current shape of Buddhism in the West. Some have brought a feminist analysis to bear on the hierarchical power structures inherent in the ancient lineages and continued in contemporary practices, and they have critiqued notions of the feminine, not as some essential set of qualities, but as culturally preferred constructions. Others have translated the earliest Buddhist wisdom texts composed by women or explored the role of early women poets in articulating their experiences of reaching enlightenment. Although Bowman references each woman's contribution, it is unfortunate that she did not include a full bibliography. Their works comprise an important body of knowledge, inquiry, and critique.

Toward the end of her introduction, Bowman states what I believe is her own manifesto.

> It is time for all of us to stop scraping and bowing before doctrines and aspects of any tradition that denies our inherent greatness. Women in particular must work to overcome thousands of years of patriarchal thinking that limit our potential. Men must strive equally hard to see through their history of privilege in the religious sphere. We must all become the Buddha we were born to be, great human beings of peace and understanding. (p. 13)

The first Noble Truth of Buddhism relates to the fact of human suffering. The second Noble Truth investigates the cause of our suffering. There is no spiritual bypass. We need to acknowledge, investigate, and pass through the sufferings of our gender—female, male, trans—in order to attain a release from suffering, though not from our gendered wisdom. Gender matters. In projecting our need and our idealizations onto a sacred image like Guanyin we see our own values reflected back to us. Cultivating tenderness, mercy, compassion, deep listening, and hearing in ourselves and for each other requires gendered work. Otherwise there is no need for a female Buddha. By contemplating the images compiled in *The Female Buddha* we open to this possibility.

# Book Reviews

Craig E. Stephenson, *Anteros: A Forgotten Myth*. London: Routledge, 2011.

REVIEWED BY JOHN BEEBE

The Jungian technique of amplification can work in two ways to open up our understanding of ancient myth. One way, developed by Jung as part of his "constructive standpoint," is to broaden the context in which a myth's images can be seen to be embedded, thereby making the myth more "ample."[1] Another, perhaps older, way is to reveal the amplitude already inherent in the myth itself by demonstrating its continuing ability to speak to experiential aspects of existence that have largely evaded conceptualization. Both kinds of amplification offer the connections revealed by a myth the chance to become conscious insights in the way we live our lives, and both are on display in Craig Stephenson's discussion of Anteros, the almost forgotten sibling of Eros,

John Beebe is a Jungian analyst in private practice in San Francisco. A past president of the C. G. Jung Institute of San Francisco, he was the founding editor of the *San Francisco Jung Institute Library Journal* (now titled *Jung Journal: Culture & Psyche*), and the first American coeditor of the *Journal of Analytical Psychology*. He is the author of numerous articles and book chapters and of the book, *Integrity in Depth*. He is coauthor, with Virginia Apperson, of *The Presence of the Feminine in Film*. Beebe is a Distinguished Life Fellow of the American Psychiatric Association.

who springs back to life in these dense, deliberate, and dazzling pages to make us wonder how we have managed to live without him.

There is scant support for a single understanding of what this god, referred to with telling ambiguity by Plato in his *Phaedrus*, may have originally portended. Each of the later literary sources—Cicero, Pausanias, Eunapius, and Themistius, whether writing in Latin or Greek—portrays the originally Attic figure of Anteros from the standpoint of a classical world dominated by Rome. Stephenson, who lets us see all the pieces he has to build on, seems to prefer the story related by the philosopher Themistius, who was based in Constantinople in the fourth century CE:

> When Aphrodite bore Eros, the lad was fair and like his mother in every way, save that he did not grow to a stature befitting his beauty, nor did he put on flesh; but he long remained at the size which he had had at birth. This matter perplexed his mother and the Muses who nursed him, and presenting themselves before Themis (for Apollo did not yet possess Delphi) they begged for a cure to this strange and wondrous mischance. So Themis spoke. "Why," said she, "I will solve your difficulty. . . . If you wish Eros to grow, you need Anteros. These two brothers will be of the same nature, and each will be cause of the other's growth." . . . So Aphrodite gave birth to Anteros, and Eros shot up at once; his wings sprouted and he grew tall. . . . But he needs his brother always beside him; sensing him large, he strives to prove himself greater, or finding him small and slight he often wastes unwillingly away.[2]

As the Titaness primarily responsible for "right order," Themis offered this solution to the oft-recognized immaturity of Eros to the goddess of love herself, Aphrodite, and to the Muses, whose ability to nurse Eros had not included the ability to guarantee his sound development. That (according to Cicero) Anteros had a different father (Ares) from any of the candidates assigned to the paternity of Eros (Stephenson seems to prefer Hermes) and that Anteros is most commonly visualized as dark suggests that the figure of Anteros, although sometimes assumed to represent "love returned," is actually the image of our aggressive shadow that likes to quarrel with love whenever it threatens to dominate our emotional life according to the formula that gives title to Caravaggio's most famous painting, *Amor Vincit Omnia [Love Conquers All]*.

From that perspective, Anteros refers to the touchy part of all of us that struggles against simply submitting to another's spontaneous affection. We turn anterotic (and thus at times away from those who love us) to embody nature's insistence that love must always be received and reflected on by the beloved before it can be returned in a way that can possibly create a relationship. Those who really love us tolerate that temporary turn from them because they realize that only if we can return it, authentically, from within ourselves may their love and ours authentically prosper. Anteros's appearance within the relational field created through an attraction spearheaded by Eros emblematizes not just resistance to Eros, but also the way Eros is enabled to become relatedness. As Stephenson argues, the anterotic response of the beloved provides the energy that can transform the lover's erotic desire into something far more mutual, and also more likely to last. Wrestling as they must in ongoing love, both partners need to be able to be both the erotic lover and the anterotic beloved.

On this foundation, Stephenson builds, in true anterotic fashion, his own counterargument to any assumption that all he is talking about is the "fulfillment of Eros." He is able to show, using literary examples from Sappho and Plato through Rimbaud and Virginia Woolf, in which he repeatedly finds Eros challenged by Anteros, that if Eros is consistently rigid in his expectations of our submission to love, Anteros is a shape-shifter whose elusive nature is changed each time a new generation takes up the effort to interpret his presence on the erotic scene.

Perhaps the most reckless countermove in the course of this history of a god who has to be continually reinterpreted to be understood at all has been the recurrent misunderstanding of the name Anteros, which etymologically means something like "love countered in reciprocal fashion." By a misguided leap of intuition, the name has too often been misunderstood to mean nothing more than anti-Eros. This unfortunate simplification is reflected in the Christian humanist distinction between profane, that is, sexual love (surely what Aphrodite's Eros had intended most humans pierced by his arrows to desire) and sacred love, the anterotic ideal of many Italian Renaissance paintings. Stephenson, developing a hint from Erwin Panofsky's analysis of Titian's *Venus Blindfolding Cupid: The Education of Love*, finds Anteros in the counter-Cupid who supports Aphrodite as she covers the eyes of the original Cupid, who apparently now needs to stop being distracted by worldly attributes to justly recognize and reciprocate love's sacred nature.[3] This is quite a distance from the imagery of Titian's *Sacred and Profane Love*, completed fifty years earlier, in which the contrasting objects of love are depicted on canvas as the nearly naked bride, innocent of persona allures, and the elegantly dressed, sophisticated married woman she is apt to become once she has profited from erotic experience.

The Christian "recuperation" of Eros as conjugal love—counting on Anteros eventually to induce Eros to outgrow even that limited permission to indulge in pagan sensuality so that humans would, at least in their mature years, finally come to appreciate love's spiritualizing aspects—experienced its own reversal in the Romantic era. As Romanticism saw it, both the Renaissance and the Reformation had left too much of the body, too much of the feminine, and even too much of evil out of what had come to pass for love in the now Enlightened, but still far too Christian world. But even Romanticism's anterotic embrace of physical passion in flight from the attempt to contain Eros within Christian marriage was to meet its own anterotic recoil. Anteros came in the modern period to refer to all the moments when lovers are not together, when they cannot meet, or when their meetings are shadowed by alienation.

Stephenson is probably at his most subtle when interpreting the content of complex, late modern contemporaries, such as the painter Francis Bacon, the poets Anne Carson, Thom Gunn, and Joseph Brodsky, the cartoonist Matt Groening (*Life in Hell*), and the filmmaker Krzystof Kieslowski (*A Short Film about Love*), all of whom have tracked how intimate relationships develop themselves not just through erotic meeting but through states of withdrawal and questioning that Stephenson accurately interprets as anterotic. As I read this section of his book I thought of the recent Academy Award–winning movie *Amour* by the great Austrian director Michael Haneke, realizing that the film develops the love between the Parisian couple, married for decades and now faced with death and separation, by giving them precisely the anterotic opportunities they need not just to test but to complete their love.

For lovers of depth psychological theory, Stephenson offers reflections on the different ways Freud, Lacan, and René Girard have configured desire, moving psychology increasingly toward the recognition of something first postulated by Hegel, that what we most desire when we desire another is the desire of that other, in other words, the anterotic completion of one's own erotic intention. Stephenson gives Jung his own chapter, making it clear that the alchemical conjunction Jung puts at the heart of the individuation process makes sense only if it is seen to emerge out of the large shadow created in any relationship by difference and unrelatedness. Although Jung understands alchemy's emphasis on the union of opposites as holding the key to the development of Eros within individuation, Stephenson pays close attention to the role played by the union of sames in the process. It is by bringing Eros as a male god into close enough relationship with his brother god Anteros that humans, both male and female, can manage to reflect on what their unions mean to their developing separate identities. Between men and women, this consciousness brings up what the individual, irreconcilable genders continue to signify. It keeps the union of same-sex partners from becoming simply a merger based on the illusion of a common identity.

Toward the end of this rich and beautifully written book, Stephenson, drawing from his work as a Jungian analyst, offers clinical vignettes of a depth and delicacy that must be read to appreciate how resonant they are to the possibilities of that aspect of the therapeutic relationship that analysts have long been taught simply to regard as "resistance." Stephenson amplifies this interactional reality, as enlarging of psychotherapy as dark energy is of the physical universe, through a fragment of the myth of Anteros that has the god wrestling with his brother Eros for the laurel of victory. The attention Stephenson gives to Anteros in the clinical setting does the service that the late James Hillman so often demanded of depth psychology: "saving" the phenomena it purports to understand. Stephenson recognizes that what analytical psychologists have always been taught to respect—the feelings, language, imagery, and interaction style that epitomize the psyche of a patient—most lets us realize our desire to help when it insists, anterotically, on its irreducible nature. This helps me to understand, as an analyst, why the patients who are most willing to receive the benefits of our love of psyche are the same ones who so stubbornly continue to present their psyches to us—as if to remind us that they love too, and in their own individual ways.

## NOTES

1. For an explanation of the constructive method or standpoint, see C. G. Jung, "On Psychological Understanding," in *The Collected Works of C. G. Jung*, vol. 3, *The Psychogenesis of Mental Disease* (Princeton, NJ: Princeton University Press, 1960), pp. 181, 184ff. For a definition of amplification, see Andrew Samuels, Bani Shorter, and Fred Plaut, *A Critical Dictionary of Jungian Analysis* (London: Routledge and Kegan Paul, 1986), pp. 16–17.

2. Themistius, *Orations*, trans., R. Pennella (Berkeley: University of California Press, 1999), p. 24, quoted by Stephenson, pp. 10–11.

3. This painting, which Titian completed when he was at least seventy-seven, hangs in the Galleria Borghese in Rome.

# BOOK REVIEWS

Astrid Berg, *Connecting with South Africa: Cultural Communication and Understanding*. College Station: Texas A&M University Press, 2012.

## REVIEWED BY ROGER BROOKE

This book comprises the sixteenth in the Carolyn and Ernest Fay Lecture Series, hosted by David Rosen and held at Texas A&M University. The title, *Connecting with South Africa*, is not only an invitation to a Jungian and international audience. Equally, Berg is describing her own response to the ethical, psychological, and political challenges for her as a privileged white South African child psychiatrist and Jungian psychoanalyst practicing in the Cape Town area. South Africa is both her own country and one from which she had been strangely excluded under apartheid until after 1994, when the new constitution was realized with the election of Nelson Mandela as the country's first democratically elected president.

Roger Brooke, Ph.D., A.B.P.P., is a clinical psychologist, professor of psychology, and director of the Military Psychological Services at Duquesne University, Pittsburgh. He is an affiliate member of the Inter-Regional Society of Jungian Analysts, author of *Jung and Phenomenology* (1991), and editor of *Pathways into the Jungian World* (1999). He is a graduate of the Universities of Cape Town, Wits, and Rhodes, and was formerly a faculty member at Rhodes University, South Africa.

The book thus marks to some extent moments in Berg's own individuation process in the context of a changing South Africa. This is not her own claim, nor is the book at all a self-indulgence. Berg models for us the multidimensional responses that white health-care workers anywhere—and not only in South Africa—are called upon to make. She does so with moral and psychological clarity, honesty, and without any of the self-absorbed and defensive "promiscuous" shame or guilt that refuses differentiation and careful thoughtfulness.[1]

Berg writes that, for her, the political changes in 1994 coincided with the requirements for deeper self-reflection and growth of a midlife transitional moment. The personal and political are intertwined. She continues: "In my European-ness I have lost my own connection to my ancestors, to a deeper universal rootedness" (p. 17). In a deep but quietly self-contained sense she is trying to find her own way home, and she is inviting us along for the journey.

Berg's access to the new South Africa is through her position as a child psychiatrist and analyst: the baby and the baby-mother couple. Babies are universally human in what they bring archetypally into the world, but they are immersed in cultural forms and meanings as soon as they engage with their mothers and are given names. The baby-mother couple is thus the point of entry for Berg into that intersection of the archetypally human and the culturally different. At the same time, this is also the occasion for coming home to one's own deepest infantile anxieties and experience of empathic failures. One cannot go there, with professional commitment and empathy as an analyst, without facing one's own history and its shadows. Berg is, of course, not specific about such history in her own life, but she touches, lightly enough, on the issues for us to appreciate what she means.

Black baby-mother couples in dreadfully socioeconomically depressed black townships are the locus for her return home—for entrance into a country which is both so familiar and close by—only a few kilometers from her university teaching hospital—and enigmatically, frighteningly strange, in which she is effectively a foreigner in her own country. It is impossible to read Berg's simple and clear narrative without an excited imagination, part of which is imagining how Berg's practical trips into Khayelitsha and Guguletu, the black townships around Cape Town, mirror a deeply interior journey into all those projections of white colonial and cultural history.

Indeed, Berg is open about the psychological challenges involved. As a white South African reader, I resonated with all the anxiety, hopes, idealizations, and folly that she herself went through. Having lived in the United States for many years now, I know that the challenges and burdens she carried are also a challenge for the almost exclusively white Jungian community, from which the absence of people of color is at least awkward.

Berg provides the reader with a sketch of our current knowledge of attachment and infant development, drawing in part from the work of analysts such as Daniel Stern, Allan Shore, Johan Norman, and Jean Knox. Berg's mentor for many years, Vera Buhrmann, was trained by Michael Fordham in the 1950s, and this tradition clearly informs her thinking. She describes in layperson's terms the links between those early maternal interactions and neurological development and points to the structural damage that occurs when there is catastrophic failure in meeting the child's needs. Two cases, both of brief, successful interventions with babies who were failing to thrive in the context of depressed mothers, are powerful and informative. They show the quality of empathic engagement required when meeting a withdrawn baby, the extent of one's own distress that must be faced and contained, and the capacity of the baby to respond to a loving adult's total engagement in body, sound, language, and facial expression. Berg does not say this explicitly, but as readers we feel called upon to face just such a challenge in ourselves as we bridge the cultural divides from dominant white culture to the black African culture that has been abused and deprived for generations under colonial rule and then apartheid. Psychological and political themes and requirements mirror each other and, in Berg's work in South Africa, are not easily separable.

These opening chapters set the ground for a case study of failure and then partial but uncertain success. I do not want to spoil the story of Athi and his mother, Nosakhele. Suffice it to say that Berg's narrative is compelling, with all the nuance and complexity one would expect from someone who has been immersed in the issues for many years. She writes of an early case, in which she was sincere, dedicated, and determined to provide the best possible First World care to a black mother and her infant. She set aside whatever prejudices that might have lingered from her earlier years growing up privileged in white South Africa. Politically liberal and well meaning, she had followed the rhetorical position of the mainstream antiapartheid struggle, which was that we are all the same as human beings, sharing rights and basic needs. (The black consciousness movement, of which Steve Biko was the best known leader, sought to correct this neglect of difference and to discuss what black African cultures could offer to the dominant politics, but it did not gain currency in white circles or the mainstream struggle, where the African National Congress set the tone.) For decades the language of cultural difference had been used oppressively. Spun with an evolutionary overlay, cultural difference was foundational for apartheid. The post-apartheid celebration that we are all one people was politically liberating and psychologically euphoric. It was also a defensive refusal of difference. Not many in those early post-apartheid years could appreciate the subtlety of Archbishop Tutu's symbol of South Africa being a "rainbow nation." If difference was acknowledged by uninformed white liberals, it was typically mixed with an idealization of traditional black cultures. With some humor, Berg describes getting conned out of a substantial amount of money in her first foray into the black townships. That was one moment marking the withdrawal of projections!

More tragically, another such moment was when the case of Athi took a stunning and life-changing turn for the worse. Nosakhele and her baby were not simply the same as white, European-rooted mothers and babies, and failure to enter into this cultural difference was what led to treatment failure. Fortunately, with long-term dedication and commitment, Dr. Berg and her team managed to follow up the story for ten years and, it seems, helped somewhat in facilitating some recovery. Through these events Berg realizes how the countertransference anxieties regarding her own history and place in this awakening country had been played out in her care of this nursing couple. As Berg writes:

> The idealization of the good black mother and the vilification that ensued [afterward] attest to the fact that we were struggling with deep collective cultural complexes: we wished not to be racist, not to be prejudiced, but in that denial of difference we achieved the opposite—we left a young woman in an intolerable situation, one in which she and her infant were nonpersons, cut off from the very fabric that would have enveloped and held them. (p. 51)

Having discussed infants, mothers, and the significance of people's names, Berg discusses the Xhosa male adolescent's rite of passage into manhood. This includes circumcision, ritual separation from the mother, a period of enduring pain and hardship without maternal intervention, and ceremonial return to the community as a man. She discusses the similarities and differences between this rite of passage and the oedipal themes made famous by Freud and understood by Jung. These discussions by Berg continue the tradition of fine writing and analysis pioneered by Vera Buhrmann, founder of the Cape of Good Hope Centre for Jungian Studies and what became the Southern African Association of Jungian Analysts.[2]

The book ends with a discussion of the Nguni term, *ubuntu* ("oo-buun-too"). The term describes a fundamental quality of being human, which both is given to us as human beings and is also a task for ethical and spiritual realization. Rooted in African humanism, it is the quality of compassion, forgiveness, and generosity that is infused throughout one's relationships with others, both living and dead, and even to our nonhuman animal cousins and the natural world at large. It is rooted in the understanding that we are only human through others. Interdependency and ethics precede any ontology of the person or selfhood. When psychological development (individuation) is imagined through the term *ubuntu,* it then involves the self-realization of the person in ever-widening circles of engagement and ethical commitment.[3] Berg works diligently to help her white, Western readers to understand this term, which defies our habitual categories and theoretical concepts. She corrects her earlier suggestion that *ubuntu* is a cultural complex, for instance.[4] She also argues that *ubuntu* does not fit into our usual sense of subjectivity, which is rooted in French and British enlightenment and located in an inner realm behind one's skin, especially within the skull.

The extraordinary humanity of persons such as Mandela and Tutu is the embodiment of *ubuntu.* Berg concludes:

> This is beyond complex theory, this is something else—what it is, and where it fits into psychological theory, remains a question. Perhaps it is best located within the traditional African religious or spiritual attitude, as indeed Mandela and others have claimed. (p. 51)

Some readers might wish for more theoretical development and integration in this little book. For instance, Berg does not take very far the question of what Xhosa adolescent manhood ritual might show white neo-Europeans about male identity and individuation through adolescence, or about the pathology of oedipal victors and the *puer* men who so regularly meet us in our consultation rooms. In a more general way, she does not go far with the questions of how Xhosa culture and relationships might inform our developmental and psychological theories. Berg certainly learns personally and clinically from Xhosa culture, and she shares those lessons with us, but what we might learn about ourselves and our theoretical assumptions is sketchy.

Berg also seems to struggle with the notion of *ubuntu* more than she might. Although the term is rooted in African sensibilities, Berg does say, following African sources, that the term describes something fundamental about being human. But if this is true, then it seems too quick to conclude that it describes something that "no longer exists in Europe" (p. 114). In fact, there have been a number of attempts in twentieth-century European philosophy to describe interdependence and its ethical ground in the ontological structure of being human. One might think especially of the work of Levinas, for instance. It is also evident in the clinical and experimental writings of the theorists Berg admires. All of them recognize that a person becomes a person through other persons (to translate a familiar Zulu and Xhosa saying) and that personhood is more of a developmental and ethical accomplishment than a given. These writings seem to offer experimental and clinical support for the concept of *ubuntu* as a fundamental structure of being human, a capacity of the self, developed or distorted, split, or repressed in one's personal and cultural development. Yet Berg does not develop this line of thinking or address the possibility of *ubuntu* as a capacity of the self. If she had, she might have gone more deeply into the question of its shadow as well.

Finally, this is not a book which looks very critically at Jung's prejudices and the way in which his colonialism formed his perceptions of Africa and its inhabitants. As has been discussed in detail by Adams, Jung's assumptions continued to form a background upon which his model of psyche, conscious and unconscious, light and dark, rational and primitive, spirit and nature, and individuation were figured.[5] While Berg's human example and clinical work show that these difficulties can be bracketed and largely transcended, I tend to think the issues cannot be avoided if any significant conceptual integration of her experience into analytical psychology is to be developed. The work of Michael Adams, just mentioned, would seem to be indispensable.

Such criticisms are unfair to the extent that they go beyond the focus and scope of Berg's book. What readers will find here is an inspiring and compelling account of a dedicated child psychiatrist and analyst bridging a great cultural and political divide, learning from and sharing her experience, and bringing to life the Xhosa persons, relationships, and some of the rituals that she encounters. She invites us to see the faces of the Xhosa across a depersonalizing history both brutal and subtle—and she manages to do this without once wagging her finger at us, her readers. This little book is a gift.

## NOTES

1. G. Straker, "Unsettling whiteness," *Psychoanalysis, Culture and Society* 16, no. 1 (2011): 11–26.

2. Vera Buhrmann, *Living in Two Worlds* (Cape Town, South Africa: Human and Rousseau, 1984).

3. Roger Brooke, "*Ubuntu* and the Individuation Process," *Psychological Perspectives* 51 (2008): 36–53.

4. Astrid Berg, "*Ubuntu*—A Contribution to the 'Civilization of the Universal,'" in *The Cultural Complex: Contemporary Jungian Perspectives on Psyche and Society*, T. Singer and S. Kimbles, eds. (New York: Brunner-Routledge, 2004).

5. Michael Adams, *The Multicultural Imagination: "Race," Color, and the Unconscious* (London: Routledge, 1996). See also Brooke, "*Ubuntu* and the Individuation Process."

# BOOK REVIEWS

Veronica Goodchild, *Songlines of the Soul: Pathways to a New Vision for a New Century*. Lake Worth, FL: Nicholas Hays, 2012.

REVIEWED BY DENNIS PATRICK SLATTERY

R eaders familiar with Veronica Goodchild's earlier work, *Eros and Chaos: The Sacred Mysteries and Dark Shadows of Love* (2001), will quickly understand *Songlines of the Soul* as a further elaboration, but by no means a repetition or a shallow makeover, of the themes in her first book. For instance, in the same engaging style with which she writes the current text, in *Eros and Chaos* she offers, in a chapter entitled "Love's Suffering," that "we are a mystery to be revealed, not only something to be known; we participate in other dimensions and

Dennis Patrick Slattery, Ph.D., is core faculty in the Mythological Studies Program at Pacifica Graduate Institute, where he has taught for the past nineteen years. He is the author, coauthor, editor, or coeditor of nineteen books, including four volumes of poetry, and dozens of articles that have appeared in journals, newspapers, and collections of essays. His most recent publications include *Day-to-Day Dante: Exploring Personal Myth through the Divine Comedy* and *Riting Myth, Mythic Writing: Plotting Your Personal Story*. Currently he is finishing a collection of essays on psyche and poetics, *Creases in Culture*, as well as a book on Herman Melville's *Moby-Dick*. He offers Riting Myth retreats at Friends of Jung groups throughout the United States and Switzerland. His website is www.dennispslattery.com.

vibrations of reality. We are, and are not, bounded by the extremities of the physical body."[1]

Now this idea that many of us have been thinking too small while missing the voices, images, and presences of other domains that would, if accepted as they are, radically alter our angle of vision on the world, as well as burst asunder so many assumptions we carry with us daily, is pushed far more broadly and deeply in *Songlines*. Clearly Goodchild has been musing on these themes consistently over a long stretch of time; in the process they have been imagined anew.

In this new study her orbit of concerns has considerably widened; perhaps the geometry of the spiral is more apt to describe the way in which she works; her imagination spirals, which as C. G. Jung reminds us is the path of all psychic development: "Psychologically, you develop in a spiral, you always come over the same point where you have been before, but it is never the same, it is either above or below."[2] *Songlines* develops its essential themes with such gracious and graceful geometry. Consider some of the chapter titles: "The Return of the Mysteries," "Anomalous Experiences and the Subtle World," "UFOs, Collective Synchronicities, and Transformation," "Crop Circles: Star Codes/Earth Dreams," "Mystical Cities and Musical Notes," "Healing Sanctuaries and Hissing Snakes," and "Eros Consciousness, Water, and the Moon: Songlines and the Return of the Cosmic Soul." As readers, we come full spiral back to her original theme, now linked intimately to presence and persistence of the cosmic soul.

As the book made its public debut, the author shared with her readers the observation that her ideas come slowly; she sensed that she needs a longer period of incubation for her ideas to come to full fruition, for the sentences to arrive when they are ready, so that the progress of this book covered many years, refusing to be rushed. One can easily attest to the ripeness, the maturity of the thought, and the daring of the author to boldly discuss UFOs and crop circles as manifestations of another order of reality that wants us to hear and see its manifestation through images that disrupt, theories that unsettle, and appearances that confuse. Yet, as an explorer, she is intrepid in turning toward any phenomena that manifest another level of consciousness or persistence in pushing themselves into presence, from the poetry of Suhrawardi, a twelfth-century mystic, to the *Tibetan Book of the Dead,* to the latest findings of quantum physics, to a dream

Goodchild experienced most recently. I am persuaded by her argument that all is of a piece if our vision can heal into a sufficient wholeness to see how the ligaments are all connected.

A guiding force for her work is the work of the Sufi scholar Henri Corbin, who introduced us to the *mundus imaginalis*. Goodchild writes: "Lying between matter and spirit, it is that world that materializes spirit and spiritualizes or 'imaginalizes,' matter, creating symbols [that link] something known with something that remains an unknown mystery" (p. 18). Both lodestar and touchstone, this intermediate realm allows the author to see with a double vision the contours of a triple domain: matter, spirit, and soul.

Goodchild's methodology, moreover, would seem to unfold in the following way throughout her study: return, retrieve, renew, report— with the last expressing her way of giving voice to the split between matter and spirit as well as evidence that there is at work in the ordinarily extraordinary reality a healing that promises a vision of gestalt, where what we see adds up to something greater than its familiar parts. The gestalt growing from these parts is what I understand to be, as she puts in her subtitle, her "new vision for a new century."

But such a view of the whole is possible if we are able "to recover the ancient way of initiation and deep shamanic-indigenous layers of the psyche that are the birthright of every human being" (p. 57). Later she reminds us what she has accomplished thus far in her travels: "how individuals are transformed by experiences that put them in touch with the Other world" (p. 97). While "otherness" became a catchphrase in literary theory several decades ago, here it is revitalized to suggest that, in the spirit of Irish fairy lore, there is behind what we see another world to be sensed through images, events, sightings that are often kept out of the conventional stream of consideration. Goodchild's intention is to retrieve these "other" experiences and pull them together into a tightly wrought version of a new contemplative vision.

I found especially engaging her discussion of UFOs, originating with Jung's own work on such unexplained phenomena, as one of those "other" events largely avoided but which Jung himself gravitated toward "in order to find the mysterious depths of meaning for which the human soul searches" (p. 142). Both they and the appearance of the majestic and delicately crafted crop circles are like signposts on a highway that few even want to admit exist, yet these images emanating from outer space and on the earth's surface have their own language and speak to us of a lost wholeness within. While contemplating one crop circle's shape, she extends its geometry to many others in suggesting that it is a "symbol of wholeness, images of the Self in matter, signaling to us that it is time to integrate our science with our religious longing and unite our earthly and heavenly natures" (p. 199).

Her own personal examples, far from detracting from her research, ground her findings in the body of her life as well as the life of the body—in dreams, synchronicities, visions, and intuitive truths that bypass the logos of the soul and connect rather with its deeper poetic impulses. I take from these explorations and recognitions the thought that many similar experiences are perhaps occurring in my own life but are too easily bypassed in favor of more rational events. *Songlines* has been a crucial guide for me in allowing experiences that are easily deflected from serious conscious consideration to become more fully present.

One must then enter *Songlines* with an open mind and heart, to allow oneself an opportunity to think and imagine differently, more wholly and poetically, for matter itself has its own elegiac voice. To enter Goodchild's landscape is to carry the poet John Keats's admonition to be comfortable in uncertainty, to cease grasping and be willing to be opened "to the union of soul and life in a revelation of love: our human love, and the love of the cosmos for us" (p. 370). Whether we call that cosmic love God, the transcendent, a benevolent universe, or simply its fundamental nature seems, at the end of her rich voyage, beside the point. Even while ensnared in an orthodoxy of seeing, the reader of this groundbreaking work can see the contours of a new order yearning to be born.

## NOTES

1. Veronica Goodchild, *Eros and Chaos: The Sacred Mysteries and Dark Shadows of Love* (York Beach, ME: Nicholas-Hays, 2001), p. 65.

2. C. G. Jung, *Dream Analysis: Notes of the Seminar Given in 1928–1930* (Princeton, NJ: Princeton University Press, 1984), p. 100.

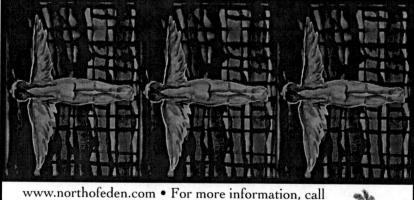

# A Joint Jung/Lacan Conference
## The Notion of the Sublime in Creativity and Destruction

### St John's College Cambridge, UK
### Friday 12th – Sunday 14th September 2014

### Lionel Bailly ♦ Bernard Burgoyne ♦ Ann Casement ♦ Phil Goss

One hundred years since the outbreak of The Great War, which radically changed many of the western world's rational values and belief systems, this conference brings together scholars and psychoanalysts from different disciplines to explore, through a depth psychological lens, the forces of creativity and destruction enshrined in the notion of the *sublime*.

Conference to include:
Keynote Lectures
Papers by Delegates
Breakout Sessions
Posters

Further details and registration forms from:
Barbara Ashworth, Jung/Lacan Secretariat
Cambridge Conferences, The Lawn, 33
Church Street, Great Shelford, Cambridge CB22 5EL, UK
Tel: +44(0)1223 847464
bm.ashworth@tiscali.co.uk

Closing date for applications 30th June 2014
(places are limited and early application is advisable)

Kindly supported by: IAAP & Spring Journal Books

# CALL FOR PAPERS
# A JOINT JUNG/LACAN CONFERENCE

**DEADLINE FOR PAPERS:** 30th September 2013
Notice of acceptance by 31st January 2014
Acceptance of the paper in the final programme is
subject to registration being made by
the presenting author before 15th May 2014

♦ Each abstract should be submitted on an A4 page
  and sent by email
♦ The abstract must contain the following information:
  Title of abstract
  Names of all authors (surname followed by initials)
  Address, telephone and email address of lead author
  Presenting author if different
  Author's clinical and academic affiliation
♦ The abstract must be in English and be limited to
  300 words
♦ Each abstract should be submitted in single spaced
  10 point Arial Font

Abstracts may be submitted via email to:
bm.ashworth@tiscali.co.uk
or by postal mail to:
Barbara Ashworth
Jung/Lacan Secretariat
Cambridge Conferences
33 Church Street
Great Shelford
Cambridge CB22 5EL UK
Tel: +44 (0) 1223 847464

Kindly supported by: IAAP & Spring Journal Books

# ENLIGHTENING CONVERSATIONS
## MAY 9-10, NEW YORK CITY 2014

### A New Series Exploring the Intersection of Buddhism & Psychoanalysis

Presented by Spring: A Journal of Archetype and Culture and the Tricycle Foundation

#### Hosted by
#### Enlightening Conversations founder and director, Polly Young-Eisendrath

## "OPPORTUNITIES AND OBSTACLES IN HUMAN AWAKENING"

"Opportunities and Obstacles in Human Awakening" will open the Enlightening Conversations series, in which psychoanalysts and Buddhist teachers will speak openly and honestly about the nitty-gritty of liberation.

Polly Young-Eisendrath ♦ Henry Shukman ♦ Pat Enkyo O'Hara Roshi ♦ Jeffrey Rubin ♦ Shoji Muramoto ♦ Pilar Jennings ♦ Robert Caper ♦ James Shaheen ♦ Grace Schireson ♦ Robert Chodo Campbell ♦ Nancy Cater ♦ Deon Van Zyl ♦ Melvin Miller ♦ Deborah Luepnitz

In an environment of trust, mutual inquiry and discovery, Enlightening Conversations will offer a series of conversational conferences in which there will be no papers read or presented. Instead, speakers will briefly introduce their subject, and then speak on a panel together in structured dialogue with each other, and the audience. Through panels and small group conversations, these conferences will engage all participants—speakers and audience—in reflective discussions about how our painful enactments and desires can be studied and transformed in an atmosphere of compassionate awakening.

The first conference, "Opportunities and Obstacles in Human Awakening," will feature principally the contributors to this issue of Spring, Buddhism and Depth Psychology: Refining the Encounter, which will be sold at the conference. The presenters are all accomplished teachers and psychoanalysts, well known in their field. They will be joined by Tricycle editor, James Shaheen, and Zen Teacher Pat Enkyo O'Hara Roshi. The three topics to be taken up are the following: (1) Awakening and Insight: Conversations About "Enlightenment" and "Being Fully Analyzed" (2) Idealization, Splitting and Projection: Conversations About Uses and Abuses of Discipline and Power (3) Humor, Helping, and Healing: Conversations About Humor, Paradox, and Helping Self and Others.

#### For more information and to register go to
## http://www.tricycle.com/conference